FREE-MARKET CAPITALISM WITH A SOUL

Capitalism and Community in the Information Age

Daryl J. Wennemann

Parma House Books
Saint Louis

Copyright © 2006 by Daryl J. Wennemann
Published by Parma House Books
7434 Williams Avenue
St. Louis, MO 63117

Cataloging-in-Publication Data
Wennemann, Daryl J., 1956-
Free-market capitalism with a soul : capitalism and community in the
Information Age / Daryl Wennemann.
p. cm.
Includes bibliographical references.
ISBN-13 9780970172341
ISBN 0970172346
1. Capitalism -- Moral and ethical aspects – United States. 2. Capitalism --
Social aspects – United States. 3. Business ethics -- United States. 4. Social
responsibility of business – United States. 5. Management -- Moral and ethical
aspects. 6. Corporate governance-- 7. Information technology -- Economic
aspects -- United States. I. Title
HB501.W46 2006
330'.12'2'0973 – dc22
Library of Congress Control Number: 2006936468

Printed on acid-free paper

Printed in the United States of America

For Cheryl

CONTENTS

Chapter I
Compassionate Conservatism: A New Ideology?

With the advent of the administration of George W. Bush we have seen a new ideology arise, that of compassionate conservatism. The ideology is so new that it is difficult to assess. Many wonder if it is a mere slogan that is intended to soften the image of the Republican Party, or something more substantial.[1] In the early months of President Bush's first administration one criticism that was leveled was that it was too beholden to business interests. One of the first steps that the administration took was to eliminate a Clinton administration rule, put in place in the last days of its tenure, which protected workers from repetitive motion injuries. As a story from the St. Louis Post-Dispatch put it, "Compassionate Conservatism apparently means compassion for the business interests who funded Mr. Bush's campaign."[2] The Bush administration also received criticism for its energy/environmental policy.[3] On the surface it seemed that the new Bush administration had a narrow vision for the country. I myself remember hearing George W. Bush say, "The business of America is business."[4]

According to its best spokespeople, the focus of compassionate conservatism was to be on the relation between government and religious groups that provide various social services. Marvin Olasky characterizes that relationship such that the government would be viewed as a clearinghouse and catalyst for the compassion of people. There are, in his view as well as that of the president, great resources of caring, decency, and commitment in the society. Compassionate conservatism is supposed to be a "fully-fledged program with a carefully considered philosophy" which has as its goal to transform America. According to Olasky, "We can make the world more welcoming. We can share our resources-both material and spiritual-with those who need them."[5]

Olasky's vision of compassionate conservatism is a conservatism that cares for the poor.[6] However, it does not wish to undermine the poor (psychologically and socially) through well-intentioned but harmful government programs that make them dependent upon an impersonal governmental largess. He gives examples of several non-governmental social aid organizations that he believes are more effective than governmental ones in providing the kind of aid that develops the abilities of persons to become independent, productive citizens. The role of the government is to provide support for these kinds of efforts that often have a faith-based orientation. The government is to equip and empower faith-based groups in their efforts to express their compassion in their local communities.

Of course, the problem that many have with this approach is that it seems to broach the traditional separation between church and state. As a result, some of those who head faith-based organizations do not want the government to be involved in their charitable efforts. They fear that the red tape usually associated with governmental support will hinder their efforts and may also require them to give up their religious orientation. The compassionate conservative wants to cut through the red tape that is usually involved in any governmental program and allow faith-based groups to pursue their religious goals as well as their social goals.

The issue of the separation of church and state is not really one that I want to take up. I am more interested in exploring the nature and extent of the compassion of the compassionate conservative, its focus and field of application. It seems to extend to the poor, but does it extend to the working poor?[7] Does it extend to the working middle class? At the same time that we have seen President Bush promoting his compassionate conservatism we have also seen a large number of workers laid off from their jobs (related to the recession of 2001).[8] I am sure that not all of the owners of those businesses are necessarily conservatives, but are conservatives who want the government to support private charities in order to aid the poor also willing to impoverish workers in order to improve the bottom line by laying them off?[9] Louis Uchitelle has written recently in this regard of the disposable American.[10] It seems that compassionate conservatism is directed exclusively to the non-market social sector. But why should it not also apply to the marketplace?

Let's consider several examples. Manuel G. Velasquez draws upon an article from the *Wall Street Journal* to illustrate how the idea of a right to due process is sometimes missing from the world of work. A few days before Christmas in 1982, the employees in the Chevrolet division of the Tarrytown, New York office were fired as a result of an investigation carried out by GM into employee fraud within the division. Twenty-Five workers, some of whom had been employed by GM for twenty years, were led through an assembly line whereby they were systematically stripped of their benefits as well as their company cars and were provided with cab fare to their home. None of them received any kind of hearing or were able to appeal the decision.[11]

This example is taken from the chapter in Velasquez's book on business ethics that deals with the corporation as a political organization. Many people have noticed that the modern corporation is structured much like the modern state. However, the rights that people in the United States enjoy as citizens they often do not enjoy as employees of companies. These rights include the right to due process, the right to privacy, freedom of conscience, the right to assemble, and the right to participate in the decision making process. Apart from the political aspect of this example, one thing it does not illustrate is the exercise of compassion. The model of compassionate conservatism is stretched when the layoffs are at one of the church groups that are supposed to provide the compassion.

> The office Christmas party this past Tuesday was a strange affair for employees of the Worker Benefit Plans of the Lutheran Church-Missouri Synod. The party had more the feel of the Last Supper. The previous Friday, the employees had gotten an e-mail from WBP President Dan Leeman. The budget for the new year had been approved, but things were very tight, the e-mail noted.
>
> The WBP is not a small operation. It takes care of benefits for some 30,000 church employees and family members. As of the beginning of last week, the WBP had 105 employees. It is located in the Lutheran-Church-Missouri Synod headquarters building on South Kirkwood.

So employees read the e-mail about the new budget, and for some, gallows humor replaced holiday cheer. How would their employer "wring" in the new year? By firing people?

The Christmas party—actually, a luncheon at the Anheuser-Busch Conference Center in Fenton—was scheduled for Tuesday. A new e-mail popped up on the computers Monday. When employees returned from the luncheon Tuesday afternoon, they were to go to the chapel for a mandatory staff meeting.

So the mood was not entirely festive at the nonalcoholic luncheon.

When the staff returned from the luncheon, they gathered in the chapel. Leeman addressed them. Seventeen people were going to be laid off, he said. The unlucky 17 would be notified the next day.

To many of the employees, it seemed a strange way to do things. Did someone in the church think there was a value or benefit to shared suffering? Because shared suffering is what it was. As the staff headed home on Tuesday, there was great uncertainty.

"I don't think many of us got much sleep Tuesday night," an employee told me.

Wednesday dawned. It was exactly one week before Christmas. The staff filed into the Lutheran-Church Missouri Synod building. They went to their desks.

The unfortunate 17 were notified. Eight were temporary workers. The others were permanent. The news was bad. These were not temporary layoffs. The positions were being eliminated. The work force is primarily female, and 16 of the 17 terminated workers were women. One had worked there for 35 years.

One nice thing about getting canned in a church headquarters building is the ready availability of pastoral counseling. A chaplain was there to talk to the terminated workers, but most declined the offer.[12]

Velasquez provides an example of another company that did show considerable compassion for its employees. It did so to such a degree that some might question whether it was a good business decision. This is the rather famous case of Aaron Feuerstein. In 1995 a fire swept through the factory owned by his family since 1906. Because most of the other textile factories in the region had left the country for the sake of finding cheap labor, Malden Mills was the largest employer in Lawrence, Massachusetts. The loss of this business would have been a fatal blow to the town and the surrounding region. Of course, many people believed Aaron Feuerstein would take the insurance money and do the same thing, move to Mexico or China. But he surprised everyone in the town and the business community when he decided to rebuild in Lawrence. The main reason for his decision was that he viewed the workers as,

> "the most valuable asset that Malden Mills has . . . not an expense that can be cut.". . .Feuerstein had refocused the company on the pricier end of the textile market where state-of-the-art technology and high-quality goods are more important than low costs. Shunning low-margin commodity fabrics such as plain polyester sheets, the company focused on a new synthetic material labeled "Polartec" that company workers had discovered how to make through trial and error during the early 1980's.[13]

Not only did Aaron Feuerstein decide to remain in Lawrence, but he informed his employees that he would continue to pay them their full salary and medical benefits while the plant was being rebuilt and that they would have their old jobs back as well.

> "I have a responsibility to the worker, both blue-collar and white-collar," Feuerstein later said. "I have an equal responsibility to the community. It would have been unconscionable to put 3000 people on the streets and deliver a death blow to the cities of Lawrence and Methuen. Maybe on paper our company is [now] worth less to Wall Street, but I can tell you it's [really] worth more."[14]

In the end, there were some workers that Malden Mills was not able to bring back. But they did help those workers with retraining and assistance in finding other work. Now, I don't know if Aaron Feuerstein is a conservative, but he certainly seems to be compassionate. He views his workers as members of the community, to which he feels a certain responsibility. In a television interview he spoke of the workers of his company as "my people."[15] Isenberg School management professor Robert Marx noted, "Without question, Aaron's compassion for his employees created an extraordinary emotional bond and feelings of intense responsibility toward one another . . . ."[16]

My question remains: why should the compassion of compassionate conservatives be restricted to the social sector? Does good business decision making require that we not express our compassion in the market? Of course, labor can be considered quite impersonally as a cost of production. And that means that laying off workers is an easy way to cut costs. It seems to be a practice that

is demanded as a sort of economic necessity. However, the statistics on mass layoffs are rather staggering:

> In May 2001, there were 1,426 mass layoff actions by employers as
> measured by new filings for unemployment insurance benefits during
> the month, according to data from the U.S. Department of Labor's Bu-
> reau of Labor Statistics. Each action involved at least 50 persons from
> a single establishment, and the number of workers involved totaled
> 157,759. (See table 1.) In January 2001 through May 2001, the total
> number of events, at 7,426, and initial claims, at 878,387, were higher
> than in January-May 2000 (5,873 and 627,520, respectively).[17]

Jeffrey E. Garten has suggested that such ill treatment of workers could have long-term deleterious effects. Garten sees Wal-
Mart as the new face of "American-style global capitalism."
While Wal-Mart does provide cheap goods which can hold down
inflation and increase profit margins, "the dark side of the story is
how Wal-Mart achieves its fabled low prices in part by taking un-
fair advantage of employees and communities."[18] The ill treatment
he points to includes hiring undocumented workers, denying workers earned overtime pay (which is one way of raising productivity),
overly restrictive health-care policies, and sexual discrimination.
Regarding communities, Wal-Mart has been accused of taking advantage of temporary tax breaks, according to Garten, and then
leaving communities in the lurch. Garten goes on to note that there
may be a backlash against such ruthless corporate behavior.

> A company that ignores its workers and its communities will surely
> have trouble succeeding in today's brand-conscious world. In addition,
> employees and citizens are consumers, too; if they are treated badly,
> their purchasing power will either erode or be directed elsewhere...in
> the contest between ruthlessly competitive forces and decent employ-
> ment in cohesive communities, we should be rooting for the latter.[19]

Garten suggests that there may be another way of treating employees that in the long run is more productive. And that is to treat
them as members of a community, and not simply as disposable
labor. That is what I would like to try to consider. Can we carry
out our economic lives in community within a capitalistic setting?
Aaron Feuerstein's example suggests that we can. Such an orientation would radically alter the work experience of people living

within capitalistic societies. As we shall see, this sense of community is precisely what is missing from the experience of persons in contemporary capitalistic societies. This was an insight that the great management theorist, Peter Drucker, had some sixty years ago. He focused on the felt loss of community in the fascist societies of the thirties and forties. He then tried to develop a lived sense of community in the market sector of the western democratic capitalist societies. This study is intended to follow up on Drucker's vision and indicate that the best practices of corporations today embody it.

There are others who have focused on the community as the locus of economic development. Place-based economic development provides a context for developing community within business organizations, as Drucker sought to do. There are a number of strategies for stabilizing local communities by investing in the development of businesses that do not tend to shift their production overseas in order to find cheap labor. It is also possible to develop strategies that allow localities to avoid a bidding war for companies to locate in their communities, only to see them move out once their tax incentives no longer hold. Such local place-based development also has the effect of strengthening democratic participation at the local level.

Overall, the impulse of the compassionate conservative to make the world a more welcoming place, as Olasky put it, is one that needs a broader field of expression. It can be applied successfully to the market as well as the non-market sector. Ethical theory supports treating business organizations as moral communities and contemporary management science has shown that a democratization of the workplace can have multiple positive outcomes within organizations.

In the next chapter we will look at Peter Drucker's search for community within a capitalistic economic setting. We will then consider the ethical foundation for making the claim that we ought to pursue a community structure in our economic lives. Immanuel Kant's ethical theory calls for the construction of a kingdom of ends that can be interpreted as a community of self-legislating persons. David Bowie has systematically applied Kant's ethical theory to business life and shows that it provides a consistent and coherent account of business ethics. In addition, Amitai Etzioni has developed a deontological approach to economics as part and parcel of his communitarian Socio-Economics. We then move on to a management theory that overcomes an obstacle Peter Drucker confronted in his search for community within business settings. Russell Ackoff's circular organization model allows for both a democratization of the workplace and the maintenance of a functional hierarchy that is seemingly required by contemporary large organizations. In the following chapter we will outline different models of high-performance organizations as illustrated in Eileen Appelbaum's treatment of the New American Workplace. In chapter six we look at the possibility of coordinating public and private investment strategies aimed at developing and maintaining strong communities. In the concluding chapter we look at the idea of a caring organization. Finally, the European Dream as outlined by Jeremy Rifkin provides an overarching perspective for understanding the compatibility of capitalism and community as a social choice that transcends economic necessity.

It is my claim that the development of an information economy brings with it the need for a social setting that is best characterized as a community. For, now the knowledge of workers is the most important asset companies possess (remember the innovation that Aaron Feuerstein's workers introduced). But the knowledge of workers is most effectively applied only in a setting of free self-direction. And this implies a democratization of the workplace. This kind of social setting is one that typically raises worker morale and productivity. If workers were allowed to share in the financial gains that follow upon a rise in productivity, we face the possibility of developing high-performance companies with high wages and good working conditions. As such, it may be that the information economy will allow us to have our economic cake and eat it too.

NOTES

1. See Robert J. Samuelson's article, "Cynical Conservatism", Washington Post, Oct. 5, 205, p. A 23,
http://www.washingtonpost.com/wp-dyn/content/article/2005/10/04/AR2005100400981.html.
2. St. Louis Post-Dispatch, March 9, 2001 p. C8. See "Big Business to Cash In?".
http://money.cnn.com/2004/11/08/news/economy/legislation_outlook/.   The business page of the St. Louis Post-Dispatch featured two stories on February 27, 2005, p. E1: "CEO bonuses rise 46.4 percent" and "Cuts may leave some out in the cold". The first story indicated that the median bonus for CEOs was 141 percent of annual salary (while their tax liability was reduced by the Bush tax cut). The second story described the cut in the federal Low-Income Home Energy Assistance Program (while the cost of natural gas has tripled in the last five years). See also, "The Road to Riches Is Called K Street,"
http://www.washingtonpost.com/wp-dyn/content/article/2005/06/21/AR2005062101632.html
3. In the January 31, 2005 edition of Time magazine, p. 43, former Bush administration EPA chief Chrisitine Todd Whitman remarks (from an excerpt of her book, *It's My Party Too*), "The Bush administration deserves credit for some important environmental measures . . . . Yet, in recent years, the Republican party's reputation as a steward of the environment has dramatically deteriorated, and the party is now widely perceived by the American public as downright anti-environment . . . Rather than forcefully and consistently making the case for more innovative environmental policies, the approach in recent years has always been to emphasize instead the party's sympathy with the concerns of business."
4. This was written before the 9-11 event.
5. Marvin Olasky, *Compassionate Conservatism*, The Free Press, 2000, p. xiii.
6. See Pat Buchanan's new book, *Where the Right Went Wrong*, Thomas Dunne Books, St. Martin's Press, 2004. Buchanan argues that there is no longer an authentic conservative party in Washington D.C.
7. See *Nickel and Dimed: On Not Getting By in America*, Barbara Ehrenreich, Owl Books, 2002.
8. For an extensive thesis on downsizing see,
http://www.geocities.com/WallStreet/Exchange/4280/.
9. See "Hewlett Packard to Lay Off 14,500 to Save $1.9", at
http://www.nytimes.com/2005/07/19/technology/19cndhp.html?hp&ex=1121832000&en=6aec6f9d46961b2&ei=5094&partner=homepage
10. Louis Uchitelle, *The Disposable American: Layoffs and Their Consequences*, Knopf, 2006.
11. Manuel G. Velasquez, *Business Ethics*, 5th ed., Prentice Hall, 2002, p. 461.

12. "Job anxiety makes Christmas party an affair to remember", Bill McClellan, St. Louis Post-Dispatch, C 1, 12-22-02.

13. Manuel G. Velasquez, *Business Ethics*, 4th ed., Prentice Hall, p. 120-121.

14. Ibid.

15. This can be seen in the ABC News/Prentice Hall Video Library, *Business Ethics*, Cassette One, Prentice Hall Inc., 1998.

16. See http://www.som.umass.edu/som/pub/cw-s01/solomon.html.

17. See http://stats.bls.gov/news.release/mmls.nr0.htm

18. Jeffrey E. Garten, "Wal-Mart Gives Globalism a Bad Name", *BusinessWeek*, March, 2004, p. 24.

19. Ibid.

Chapter II
Historical Background for the Communitarian Ideal:
Peter Drucker's Search for Community[1]

Technological optimists think that computers will reverse some of this social atomization, touting virtual experience and virtual community as ways for people to widen their horizons. But is it really sensible to suggest that the way to revitalize community is to sit alone in our room, typing at our networked computers and filling our lives with virtual friends?[2]

Introduction

Peter Drucker is widely known for his work in management theory. His many publications in this area are well known to business students around the world. Some of his most prominent works in management theory include *The Practice of Management, Managing for Results, The Effective Executive, Managing in Turbulent Times, The Frontiers of Management, Managing for the Future,* and *Management: Tasks, Responsibilities, Practices.* These works and others have certainly placed Peter Drucker at the forefront of the study of management theory. But there is, in addition to these works, a wide range of works that may not be as widely known by those who read Drucker for the insight he brings to the practice of management. Among his nearly thirty books are works dealing with economics, politics, and social theory, as well as two novels and an autobiography under the title, *Adventures of a Bystander.*

Here I want to focus on the theme of community in Drucker's social thought. This theme, I believe, is one that runs through many of Drucker's books and may provide a central organizing theme for understanding his social thought. I believe that Drucker has tried to think about life in a capitalistic economic setting in terms of the idea of community. And this approach is one that may contribute to curing some of the ills associated with contemporary capitalism.

In a recent work, *Post-Capitalist Society*, Peter Drucker describes a felt sense of community as being an important benefit associated with voluntary work, and the work experience associated with nonprofit organizations. Drucker's argument is that this sense of community is vital to our post-capitalist society, a society that is dominated by the demands of information. So, a post-capitalist society is not necessarily socialistic or communistic, as the Marxists would say, but, according to Drucker, it is a market economy that is no longer dominated by the traditional forms of capital. Rather, information is now central to the economy.

In my view, the concern to establish a basis for community in the economic lives of persons is a constant theme of Drucker's reflections on the role of management in modern societies. The roots of Drucker's notion of community can be traced to a very early work, *The End of Economic Man*, in 1939. In this book, Drucker introduced the notion of *status*, which is a basic value that accrues to all persons who are members of a community, including workers. The status of the worker implies that workers should be treated as free persons and not merely as a means of production. This may be seen as a precursor to contemporary theories of participatory management that recognize the right of workers to participate in decision making within the workplace because they are members of a moral community or simply because they are enfranchised in some way.

As we shall see, Drucker's search for community in the economic life of modern societies was frustrated by the bifurcation of the decision-making function between management and labor. His recent reflections have led him to locate community in the nonprofit sector of our post-modern economy that has developed on the basis of a knowledge economy.

The significance of this theme can be seen in a study by Robert Nisbet, *The Quest for Community*. Nisbet has argued that much of modern thought revolves around the experience of a loss of community and a concomitant search for community. His study is an important point of departure for any study of community. This is certainly true of our analysis of Drucker's work. The loss of community and the search for community is a noteworthy theme in his thought that has not been widely recognized and accorded the significance it deserves. I hope to point to this significant theme and show how Drucker's thought itself illustrates a loss of community and a subsequent search for community.

The Quest for Community

In *The Quest for Community*, Nisbet argues that the development of modern culture is characterized by a felt loss of community and a concomitant search for community. The loss of community in modern societies has resulted, in Nisbet's view, from the rise of the modern nation-state. The modern state has taken on many of the functions of the intermediate social groups, like the family, church, guild, and other local associations that have traditionally mediated between the individual and the state. Having lost any significant social function, these traditional associations have atrophied, leaving the individual standing alone facing the virtually unlimited power of the modern state. This, in turn has given rise to the peculiar condition of alienation of the modern individual. The incoherence of social existence is correlated with the individual's sense of powerlessness in the face of the unlimited power of the state. As Nisbet has written,

I believe . . . that the single most impressive fact of the twentieth century in Western society is the fateful combination of widespread quest for community—in whatever form, moral, social, political—and the apparatus of political power that has become so vast in contemporary democratic states. That combination of search for community and existing political power seems to me today, just as it did twenty years ago, a very dangerous combination. For, the expansion of power feeds on the quest for community. All too often power comes to resemble community, especially in times of convulsive social change and of widespread preoccupation with personal identity, moral certainty, and social meaning. This is . . . the essential tragedy of modern man's quest for community. . . . The structure of political power which came into being three centuries ago on the basis of its eradication of medieval forms of community has remained—has indeed become ever more—destructive of new forms of community.[3]

Nisbet argues that human freedom is ultimately grounded in human community and the development of community in the modern age requires the development of new forms of intermediate social groups that can mediate between the individual and the state. The strategy of compassionate conservatives in focusing on faith-based organizations could be seen as an attempt to strengthen this intermediate social sphere. This is the real significance of Peter Drucker's attempt to locate community in the economic sphere. Drucker's insight is that the modern corporation may provide a social function beyond that of merely producing goods and services within a market that is made up of atomic individuals. Rather, it may provide a context for community among individuals as they carry out their economic tasks. As Drucker notes in *Technology, Management, and Society*,

> It is the organization which is today our most visible social environment. The family is "private" rather than "community"—not that this makes it any less important. The "community" is increasingly in the organization, and especially in the one in which the individual finds his livelihood and through which he gains access to function, achievement, and social status.[4]

The Status of the Individual

In 1939 Drucker wrote the first of a series of works that attempted to define the newly emerging economic environment associated with modern management. In *The End of Economic Man* (1939), Drucker analyzed fascist economies, especially those of Germany and Italy, in order to ascertain how they operated and how they differed from the economies of the Western democracies. It is interesting to note that fascism arose, according Drucker, as a result of the collapse of the Western ideal of human nature as "Economic Man". According to this ideal, the economic sphere of human activity is of the highest significance, inasmuch as it was supposed to produce both freedom and equality. It was only when the ideal failed to produce these expected results that Western people turned to fascism with the hope that it would provide equality and security, if not freedom. According to Drucker:

Through the collapse of Economic Man the individual is deprived of his social order, and his world of its rational existence. He can no longer explain or understand his existence as rationally correlated and co-ordinated to the world in which he lives; nor can he co-ordinate the world and the social reality to his existence. The function of the individual in society has become entirely irrational and senseless. Man is isolated within a tremendous machine, the purpose and meaning of which he does not accept and cannot translate into terms of his experience. Society ceases to be a community of individuals bound together by a common purpose, and becomes a chaotic hubbub of purposeless isolated monads.[5]

The import of Drucker's analysis in terms of the problematic Nisbet set out is that Drucker sees the economic order as having taken priority over other social spheres in the age of Economic Man. As such, it could provide the setting for a new form of community.

Drucker's study of fascism is significant because, according to his interpretation, the Second World War represented a historical test or experiment that would determine if the worker has status, and is thus a member of a free community, or is merely a factor of production or industrial slave. Fascist societies were really non-economic societies in the sense that economic activity, like investment and gaining profit, were subordinated to non-economic goals. In particular, the goal of fascist economies was a condition of full employment. As such, a basic lesson of the Great Depression, according to Drucker, is that economic security is a social goal that is more important to people than other economic goals. The task of the post-war Western societies would thus be to develop a new non-economic society that is able to structure human life in such a way that freedom and equality are experienced in concrete terms in the economic activities of individuals. As Drucker asserts in *The End of Economic Man*,

The next decade will decide whether Europe can find such forces which would lead her out of the impasse into which the collapse of Economic Man has maneuvered her, or whether she has to grope her way through the darkness of totalitarian fascism before she finds a new, positive non-economic concept of Free and Equal Man.[6]

Drucker holds that the new non-economic society would be an industrial society that is characterized by a new system of management that would produce a level of rationality that was undreamed of in the economic society of the eighteenth and nineteenth centuries. In *The Future of Industrial Man* (1942), Drucker extends the analysis of the previous study, arguing that Nazism represents a challenge to Western industrial culture,

> Unless we realize that the essence of Nazism is the attempt to solve a universal problem of Western civilization—that of the industrial society—and that the basic principles on which the Nazis base this attempt are also in no way confined to Germany, we do not know what we fight for or what we fight against. We must know that we fight against an attempt to develop a functioning industrial society on the basis of slavery and conquest. Otherwise we would have no basis for our own attempt to develop not only a functioning but a free and peaceful industrial society.[7]

It is clear that the non-economic values that are to guide policy making in an industrial society are, for Drucker, freedom and equality. But this means that workers must be treated as free persons having status. And this implies, in turn, that workers must somehow participate in the decision making process within the industrial order. In other words, an industrial order that is both functional and free must be conceived as being an industrial community. Such a social order must balance the demand of the individual to be recognized as having value within the group and the demand of the group that the needs of the individual should be aligned with its requirement to function effectively. The only way that the categories of status and function can be coordinated is by establishing the citizenship of the worker within the industrial order. Drucker developed this problematic to a high degree in *The New Society* (1949):

> 'Status' defines man's existence as related in mutual necessity to the organized group. 'Function' ties his work, his aspirations and ambitions to the power and purposes of the organized group in a bond that satisfies both individual and society. . . . Together status and function resolve the apparently irresolvable conflict between the absolute claim of the group—before which any man is nothing in himself and only a member of the species—and the absolute claim of the individual, to

whom the group is only a means and a tool for the achievement of his own private purpose. Status and function overcome this conflict by giving citizenship to the individual.

Man must have status and function in his society in order to be a person. . . . But the group's own cohesion and survival also depend on the individual's status and function; without it the group is a mere herd, never a society. And only a society that gives status and function to its members can expect their allegiance. Status and function of the individual member are requirements of individual and social life . . . *The concrete society of the West has to demand of the industrial enterprise that it fulfill that promise of status we call Justice, which is expressed by the slogan of 'equal opportunities'; and that it organize function according to the belief in the Dignity of Man as it is expressed in the responsible participation of citizenship.*[8]

Such a social order can be seen clearly by contrast with the Nazi social order that is founded on slavery. Even after the war against fascism was won, Drucker found that there remained the task of building an industrial civilization. Such a civilization would recognize the value of the individual worker in a concrete way within the organization of the industrial enterprise, just as the political state recognizes the value of the individual citizen. Even within a democratic political order, individual workers could very well find themselves as industrial slaves if their only role was that of a cog in the machinery of the industrial plant. In *The Future of Industrial Man*, Drucker saw that the end of the Second World War would give rise to a need for a new industrial civilization,

WE DO not today have a functioning industrial society. We have a magnificent technical machine for industrial production, built and run by engineers, chemists, and skilled mechanics. We have a considerably weaker but still very impressive economic machine for the distribution of industrial goods. Politically and socially, however, we have no industrial civilization, no industrial community life, no industrial order or organization. It is this absence of a functioning industrial society, able to integrate our industrial reality, which underlies the crisis of our times.[9]

Drucker's goal, then, was to develop a legitimate industrial social order. Just as the power of the state in a free society must be legitimate, inasmuch as it flows from the consent of the people, Drucker holds that the power of the corporation must be legitimate. And the legitimacy of the power of the corporation depends upon the recognition of the status of the worker as a sort of citizen within the economy, having rights that limit the power of the corporation.

> If the individual is not given social status and function, there can be no society but only a mass of social atoms flying through space without aim or purpose. And unless power is legitimate there can be no social fabric; there is only a social vacuum held together by mere slavery or inertia.[10]

The status and function of the individual integrates the individual into the group and makes the actions of the individual cohere with those of the group. Status and function provide for the social cohesion of modern societies that tend to lack any of the traditional social bonds of pre-industrial societies.

In *The New Society*, Drucker posits status and function as values that can lead to a free and equal society in an industrial form of federal republic. It is significant, in this regard, that Drucker has written of the plant community in order to establish a social context within which the status and function of the individual can be expressed. This represents a response on Drucker's part to the dangers inherent in the industrial mode of social production, and thus organization. As Drucker notes in *The New Society*, "Research and analysis . . . *indicates that the individual can be given status and function in the industrial enterprise.* They disprove the popular belief that the industrial system is by its very nature destructive of human community and individual dignity."[11]

One of the dangers associated with mass production is that the worker invariably becomes divorced from the means of production. For, as Drucker argues, the organization is productive in modern industrial societies, not individuals alone.[12] It is very unusual that individuals work alone in contemporary societies. The vast majority of workers today depend upon organizations for their livelihood. But within the organization, workers can be easily replaced. The separation of workers from the means of production that results from individuals being effectively reduced to a replaceable cog in the productive machinery (including the social system of organizations) threatens the status and prestige system of traditional groups and tends to dissolve the traditional community, uprooting the individual in the process. The plant community is supposed to make up for this loss.

Another danger associated with mass production is the concentration of power with the concomitant loss of individual liberty. The individual becomes subject to the impersonal forces of the market, which might leave her unemployed and thus separated from one of the primary sources of social contact. Anyone who has been caught in the wave of downsizing in recent years can undoubtedly identify with these dangers. Drucker argues that the most significant long-term effect of unemployment is psychological rather than physical. It can produce a loss of self-respect, loss of initiative, and even lead to suicide. While Drucker's analysis in *The New Society* is focused on the Great Depression, it seems to apply very well to the current environment of downsizing or rightsizing. The effect on the individual is the same no matter what it is called. According to Drucker:

> Denied access to the organization without which, in an industrial society, nobody can be productive, the unemployed becomes an outcast whose very membership in society has been suspended. It is no accident that the "depression shock" was by no means confined to those who actually suffered long-term unemployment, but hit fully as hard the men who never, during the Depression, were out of a job, and who may never have been in real danger of losing their job. For a decade they lived in the constant fear of being fired the next payday; to become actually unemployed may well have been more bearable than to go on living in constant terror.[13]

Is this not the condition of many if not most people today? They live in constant fear of being fired at any moment. A recent article in Fortune magazine described the plight of people who are in their 50's and find themselves fired.

> What's changed . . . is that discarded executives of a certain age may never find that new position...Even if you're gainfully employed, uncomfortable questions are probably swimming around in your mind. Are you vulnerable? What would you do if you got the sack and couldn't find a new gig? . . . There is always an extra layer of stress. Today, [says Grant Anderson] "being employed is an illusion".[14]

There is evidence that there are significant physical effects as well. "Loss of a work network removes an important source of human support. As a result, psychosomatic illnesses, anxiety, worry, tension, impaired interpersonal relations, and an increased sense of powerlessness arise."[15] Kathryn Marie Dudley's account of a plant closing in Kenosha, Wisconsin supports Drucker's concern in *The New Society*,

> When a plant closes, workers lose a social structure in which they have felt valued and validated by their fellows. When they are stripped of their workplace identities, dislocated workers face an external culture that no longer seems to value, or grant social legitimacy to, the kind of work they do…and when their plant closes this accumulated cultural capital is lost. Long and respectable work histories are suddenly worthless, and workers are faced with the prospect of starting all over again, from scratch.[16]

Within an industrial order the individual seems to face impersonal market forces that are as irrational as the individual who lives in a dictatorship. One is powerless before the whims of a distant ruler who determines one's fate. According to Drucker's analysis, this situation is really unbearable for the individual and threatens to undermine the functioning of an industrial society. As Drucker states in *The New Society*:

> The citizen can neither control nor understand the forces that threaten to cast him out from society and deprive him of his effective citizenship. Unless modern industrial society can banish these forces, it will not be acceptable or rational to its members. It must become instead meaningless, insane and demon-ridden, and turn into an obsessive nightmare.[17]

These dangers arise in an industrial society when purely economic goals come to predominate in our decision-making. Drucker argues that the social goals of freedom and equality must lead to a decentralization of power within the economy, and within the corporation in particular. Since the large enterprise is the organizing principle of our society, it is the real locus of freedom and equality. And so, the decision making process of large enterprises must not be swallowed up into the state. Local self-government within the economic sphere is essential in an industrial society.

The difficulty we continually face is that it seems that we must sacrifice freedom for function or function for freedom. By describing the modern corporation as a plant community, Drucker hoped to develop a mode of organization that is both functional and free.

According to Drucker, the enterprise today is both an economic and governmental or political institution. As a plant community, the enterprise discharges social functions, not just economic ones. The members of the plant community are, in a sense, citizens having the rights and obligations associated with citizenship within the state. In Drucker's words, "the plant community is a real community, indeed . . . it is the community which appears to the member of the enterprise as the representative and decisive one for the fulfillment of his social aspirations and beliefs."[18] This is confirmed in Francis Fukuyama's study of trust:

> In developing capitalist countries with strong civil societies . . . the economy itself is the locus of a substantial part of social life. When one works for Motorola, Siemens, Toyota, or even a small family dry cleaning business, one is part of a moral network that absorbs a large part of one's energies and ambitions. . . . There is no lack of divisive ethnic conflicts in these places, whether over competing Polish and Lithuanian claims to Vilnius or Hungarian irredenta vis-a-vis neighbors. But they have not flared up into violent conflicts yet because the economy has been sufficiently vigorous to provide an alternative source of belonging.[19]

In order to foster the social aspect of the enterprise Drucker notes that all members of the plant community must have a managerial attitude toward their work and toward the enterprise. For, the modern enterprise requires the active participation of every member to efficiently accomplish its tasks. In this regard, Drucker asserts that the social and moral incentives to increased productivity must be emphasized over the financial ones.[20]

Unfortunately, the need for workers to adopt a managerial attitude does not close the rift between management and labor. The central conflict of the modern industrial enterprise is the functional requirement to count the labor of workers as a cost of production, a factor of production. And this seems to be inconsistent with the status of the individual. It is important to notice that Drucker considered the policy of laying off workers in times of recession to be a sort of economic necessity. But it is a requirement of the organization that undermines their social status within the organization. When a worker is laid off, they not only lose their source of income, but an important source of social contact as well.[21]

While Drucker holds that every individual in a firm must have a managerial attitude, his study, *Concept of the Corporation*, indicates that it is a functional or structural requirement of the modern enterprise to restrict the decision making power of workers to their own particular sphere of activity.

> Decentralization as a principle of industrial order can be applied only where there is at least a rudiment of genuine executive functions. It cannot possibly be the basis for an integration of the worker into industrial society; for it is almost in the definition of the industrial worker that he does not direct but is directed.[22]

There is thus a divide between management and labor which seems to undermine the sense of community Drucker wants. This is a recurring problem in Drucker's thought that undermined his effort at developing a living plant community that fosters freedom and equality. In *The New Society*, Drucker suggests that the worker is only able to exercise a managerial function within the social sphere of the plant community, not in the economic sphere.[23] But the economic sphere of the plant community would seem to be decisive. It does not seem that the social aspect of the person's experience in the plant community can or should be divorced from the economic aspect of that experience. Drucker, however, sees such a divorce as a structural requirement of the modern industrial organization. In the end, Drucker sees the managerial attitude as being necessary to reconcile the individual to the impersonal economic necessities that drive decision making within the plant community.[24]

The market economy thus gives rise to certain economic demands that appear to be inimical to community. Do temporary and part-time employees have status within the economy? Or, are they merely disposable factors of production? As long as Drucker dealt with the problems of the market economy, there seemed to be no way for him to find a real community within the confines of the economic laws that drive economic decisions. Within the economic sphere of the plant community, the worker is not to direct but only to be directed.

On the other hand, what is the basis of the power of the managerial elite? Within an industrial civilization the power of management must be seen as legitimate, just as the power of the political elite is legitimate. Since the famous study of Berle and Means in 1932, *The Modern Corporation and Private Property*, we have known that the traditional foundation for the legitimacy of management power, i.e., ownership, is no longer valid. Do the high executive salaries we see in contemporary corporations represent a commitment to community life, especially in light of the concomitant tendency to downsize companies for the sake of short-term profitability? Here Drucker suggests that a profit-sharing plan for workers must be instituted alongside a profit-sharing plan for executives. Understood as a community, the industrial plant must make sure that the workers see themselves as being engaged in a shared undertaking with management.[25]

It is significant that in 1949 Drucker saw that in the new society it is the skills of the worker that represent the primary resource of modern industrial firms. This is a common insight in today's knowledge economy, and it may point to a significant development in the social status of individuals. In *The New Society*, Drucker suggested that the wages paid to workers should be considered as an investment in the development of their skills.[26] This is one reason that the Japanese have tended to hold on to their workers. Drucker notes that this has been part of their social contract since the end of the Second World War. But it is a practice that has begun to break down in recent years.[27] As such, they will have to develop a new social contract, one that recognizes the social needs of workers as well as their economic needs.

Community in Post-Capitalist Society

I have said that the pressures of the market economy introduced a seemingly irreconcilable split in the modern industrial plant that tended to undermine Drucker's effort to develop a sense of community within the economic sphere. In Drucker's recent books we can see a new effort to promote the importance of community within the economic lives of persons within the newly emergent world economy. It is significant that Drucker has turned to the nonprofit sector of the economy to find a role for the modern manager in building community life. In *Post-Capitalist Society* (1993), Drucker observes how significant the nonprofit sector has become in the present knowledge economy. In such an economy, of course, the skills of the worker become of primary importance to economic performance. Indeed, Drucker wants to rethink all of the economic categories like investment, savings, profit, productivity, etc., in terms of knowledge rather than the traditional notion of capital. But he also wants to promote the possibility of community within the post-capitalist enterprise.

> In the West, the plant community never took root. I still strongly maintain that the employee has to be given the maximum responsibility and self-control—the idea that underlay my advocacy of the plant community. The knowledge-based organization has to become a responsibility-based organization.
>
> But individuals, and especially knowledge workers, need an additional sphere of social life, of personal relationships, and of contribution outside and beyond the job, outside and beyond the organization, indeed, outside and beyond their own specialized knowledge area.[28]

Drucker sees the primary locus for community in post-capitalist society as lying in the many voluntary efforts of individuals who build community not on the basis of economic necessity but on the initiative of persons actively responding both to the needs of their society and their own need for commitment and a sense of belonging.

> Every developed country needs an autonomous, self-governing social sector of community organizations—to provide the requisite community services, but above all to restore the bonds of community and a sense of active citizenship. Historically, community was fate. In post-capitalist society and polity, community has to become commitment.[29]

This comports very well with the focus of the compassionate conservatives on the non-profit social sector. Their interest is undoubtedly to develop the sources of community to be found in this sector as a way of limiting and even shrinking the influence of the state in the lives of individuals.

The ultimate significance of the post-capitalist knowledge society is, according to Drucker, that it "puts the person in the center"[30], in the sense that, "The educated person now matters."[31] The educated person now matters in post-capitalist society because it is a knowledge society. As such, the educated person must carry out two roles. One is that of an intellectual (having specialized skills) and the other that of a manager, "who focuses on people and work."[32]

Of course, from a moral perspective, all persons matter because they have the status of a person as a member of a moral community. The management perspective that Drucker has consistently adopted tends to recognize the status of persons who have a managerial function. Thus, Drucker tried to extend the managerial function to non-managers, the common workers of the so-called plant community. Still, he could never overcome the division between the functional economic needs of the organization and the needs of workers that include both economic and social needs. While the business organization is mainly concerned with the production of goods, workers are concerned with their status as citizens within the organization.[33] This is why Drucker eventually turned to the nonprofit sector of the economy in order to find organizations whose functional economic requirements are not in conflict with the social needs of their workers. My view is that there is a moral imperative to recognize the status of all persons within or without the market economy, even those who are merely part-time employees, or temporary employees, or unemployed persons.

One danger of the new knowledge society is the one that Sherry Turkle described. We may tend to shut ourselves up in our own rooms and restrict our experience of community with others to the virtual relationships of the internet. Another danger is that we may tend to shut out those who do not enjoy the franchise of knowledge necessary to participate in the post-capitalist society.

However we experience community in the twenty-first century, we can find a broad and deep reflection on the problems of community in the thought of Peter Drucker. His notion of the status and function of the worker as a basis for community within the economic sphere introduces a challenge to us all: can we develop a real concrete community life that has as its goals values that are worthy of our Western heritage, i.e., the freedom and equality of persons? My contention is that the way to do this is to extend community from the non-profit sector to the for-profit sector. This is the challenge that is faced not only by the so-called compassionate conservatives, but by all of us together.

NOTES

1. This chapter is a modified version of an essay originally published under the title, "The Future of Work and the Worker: Peter Drucker's Search for Community," The Halcyon Series, *Western Futures*, vol. 22, Jan., 2000, pp, 125-140.

2. Sherry Turkle, *Life on the Screen*, New York: Simon & Schuster,1995, p. 235.

3. Robert Nisbet, *The Quest for Community*, New York: Oxford University Press, 1977, pp., vii-vii.

4. Peter Drucker, *Technology, Management, and Society*, New York: Harper & Row, 1970, p. 35.

5. Peter Drucker, *The End of Economic Man*, New York: The John Day Company, 1939, p. 55.

6. Ibid., p. 268.

7. Peter Drucker, *The Future of Industrial Man*, New York: The John Day Company, 1942, p. 19.

8. Peter Drucker, *The New Society*, New York: Harper & Row, 1962, p. 151.

9. Peter Drucker, *The Future of Industrial Man*, New York: The John Day Company, 1942, p. 21.

10. Ibid., pp., 25-26.

11. Peter Drucker, *The New Society*, New York: Harper & Row, 1962, p. 165.

12. Ibid., p. 6.

13. Ibid., p. 8.

14. *Fortune*, May 16, 2005, pp., 80, 83.

15. Bary Bluestone and Bennett Harrison, "Jobs, Income and Health", in Paul D. Staudohar and Holly E. Brown, *Deindustrialization and Plant Closure* (Lexington, MA: Lexington Books, 1987). Quoted by Thad Harrison et al., in *Making a Place for Community*, Routledge, 2002, p. 3.

16. Kathryn Marie Dudley, *The End of the Line: Lost Jobs, New Lives in Postindustrial America,* Chicago: University of Chicago Press, 1994, p. 134. Cited in Thad Harrison et al., in *Making a Place for Community*, Routledge, 2002, p. 4.

17. Peter Drucker, *The New Society*, New York: Harper & Row, 1962, p. 8.

18. Ibid., p. 49.

19. Francis Fukuyama, *Trust*, p. 361. Quoted in Norman Bowie, *Business Ethics*, p. 169.

20. Peter Drucker, *The New Society*, New York: Harper & Row, 1962, p. 49.

21. Ibid., p. 77-78.

22. Peter Drucker, *The Concept of the Corporation*, New York: Mentor Books, 1972, p. 149.

23. Peter Drucker, *The New Society*, New York: Harper & Row, 1962 p. 287

24. Ibid., p. 288.

25. Ibid., p. 252.

26. Ibid., p. 87.

27. See Peter Drucker, "Japan: The Problems of Success", *The Ecological Vision*, Transaction Publishers, 1993, pp. 381-396.

28. Peter Drucker, *Post-Capitalist Society*, New York, HarperBusiness, 1993, p. 174.

29. Ibid., p. 178.

30. Ibid., p. 210.

31. Ibid., p. 211.

32. Ibid., p. 215.

33. Peter Drucker, *The New Society*, New York: Harper & Row, 1962, p. 282.

Chapter III
Capitalism & Good Will

In his study of the historical rise of capitalism, *The Making of Economic Society*, Robert Heilbroner undertakes an extensive survey of human economic activity reaching back into prehistoric times. At the end of that study, Heilbroner speculates that the economic problem facing us in the future will no longer be survival, or simply economic growth. Rather, he suggests "the central problem which is likely to confront the societies of tomorrow is nothing less than the creation of *a new relationship between the economic aspect of existence and human life in its totality.*"[1] This is the insight Drucker had in the 1930's as he surveyed the newly emerging fascist societies. Both of them have approached "the economic problem" at a philosophical level. They both suggest the need for a sort of philosophy of economic life. Consider Heilbroner's closing remarks,

As we have already remarked, a market society does not cope easily with this choice of social opportunities. Its established mechanism continues to direct human energies into the accustomed economic channels. Thus the danger exists that the market system, in an environment of genuine abundance, may become an instrument which liberates man from real want only to enslave him to purposes for which it is increasingly difficult to find social and moral justification. . . . It is man who must then govern things rather than things which must govern man.

It is with such a vista—at once hopeful and problematic—that we leave our historic survey of the market system. Looking not only backward to the past, but forward to the very limit of our historic visibility, we can see the market system itself as groping toward an ultimate transcendence of economics as a fetter on mankind.

Now there can be seen the prospect of a final stage of economic development—a stage in which the making of economic society, as a painful struggle, comes to an end. For the first time, an orderly and generous solution to the economic problem begins to approach within human capability. The great question will then be whether men will use their triumph over nature to achieve a much more difficult victory over themselves.[2]

There are two points that are particularly striking. One is the issue of moral justification. Economists tend to avoid the whole area of moral justification as lying outside the domain of economic science.[3] As we shall see shortly, Amitai Etzioni places moral considerations at the center of his new approach to economics. The second point is Heilbroner's fascinating reference to "a generous solution." This harkens back to Olasky's assertion that compassionate conservatism seeks to make the world more welcoming. But now it is a matter of making the world of the economic market more welcoming.

Amitai Etzioni's Socio-Economics

Over the last two decades Amitai Etzioni has carried out a reflection of philosophical dimensions that seeks to found economic life in the broader totality of human existence. His communitarian approach establishes a moral and social scientific justification for making the economic world more welcoming.

The title of Etzioni's major work in this area is *The Moral Dimension*. Its subtitle is, *Toward a New Economics*. His sociological orientation, which he calls Socio-Economics, provides a much-needed antidote to the narrow utilitarian approach that is typical of mainstream economic analysis. His central insight is that among the many desires people express in the economic order is the desire to do what is morally right. As Etzioni says in the preface of *The Moral Dimension*, "The finding that people have several wants, including the commitment to live up to their moral values, and that these wants cannot be neatly ordered or regulated by prices, provides a starting point that is fundamentally different from that of the neoclassical premises."[4]

This insight explains very well the kind of decision that Aaron Feuerstein made. He took into account the effect his decision would have on his community. It may also explain the impetus behind the notion of compassionate conservatism. My point is that there is a place for compassion in the market economy if we see the market as existing within a broader context of human striving.

Etzioni argues that far from being narrow rational utility maximizers, individuals depend upon various normative/affective factors in everyday decision-making, including both the desire to pursue happiness (utility) and the desire to do their moral duty. These two sets of desires codetermine each other. He notes that often companies do not act in a way that maximizes utility. "Large amounts of research have shown that firms do not pursue one overarching goal, but that they have mixed goals; they do not maximize any one utility, and are internally divided rather than acting in unison. . . ."[5] This cannot be very well explained from the traditional neo-classical perspective. It makes perfect sense, however, from the perspective of Etzioni's socio-economics. Robert Heilbroner notes that the impetus for socially acceptable behavior on the part of business executives may be a certain guilty conscience at being viewed the way neoclassical economics says they should. "One of the problems of the theology of capitalism is that capitalists do not like to act like the creatures of pure self-interest that they are supposed to be."[6] A counter-example is provided by Norman E. Bowie. When Merk found a cure for river blindness, the company provided the drug for free to the people needing it in Africa and South America because they were too poor to be able to afford it.[7]

The element that is missing from the neoclassical economic analysis is just the social bonds that exist between people and that form the context for their economic interactions. Etzioni points out that most people recognize limits to economic competition that are moral. For example, most business people would not kill their competitor in order to gain an advantage in the market. Businesses often make charitable contributions because they feel they have a social obligation to do so. Many businesses today ask their employees to volunteer in the community. These are perhaps examples of what Etzioni calls the "hidden bases of competition." As Etzioni puts it,

> The perfect competition model assumes that the relations among the actors are impersonal, as the actors proceed independently of one another

in an anonymous market...And each actor is out to maximize what he or she can gain. This orientation is not problematic in the neoclassical paradigm of perfect competition because it is assumed that self-interest will sustain the system. It is problematic, however, in other paradigms, which acknowledge conflict, recognize the significance of positive, mutually supporting *social* bonds, and in which actors treat each other as persons, as ends, and care for one another, as contributing to the continuity of *economic* relations.[8]

It looks as if Etzioni has read Aaron Feuerstein's mind. Or, perhaps Feuerstein has read Etzioni's book. Either way, we can see in Etzioni's work a way to situate economic activity within a broader context of human striving by recognizing the social context of our economic existence. This is one reason The Marriott Corporation gave for hiring some six thousand welfare recipients. The company saw it as a way of helping the local community to develop.[9] Edwin A. Murray Jr. makes a similar point in his study on Ethics and Corporate Strategy,

I submit that companies have a role to play in striving for social justice. If inflation, gaping disparities in income distribution, poor schooling, racial tension, high crime rates, and government corruption characterize a political economy, business firms--like every other societal institution--will suffer. Working to ameliorate such conditions can pay long-term dividends in the form of larger more stable markets which are also both more sophisticated and more affluent.[10]

Etzioni points out how social bonds affect labor relations, for example. He notes that labor relations can be expected to be much more harmonious where people see themselves as a WE rather than merely a conglomeration of I's. He also notes that where social bonds are very strong, as between family members, economic competition is reduced. So, family members might find it difficult to charge each other for goods or services. And thus, we do not tend to find competitive markets in small tribal societies.[11]

Etzioni's approach lies mid-way between this sort of pre-capitalist economy and the hyper-individualistic capitalism characterized in the neoclassical account of modern economies that depends upon maximizing utility. There is, in other words, an intermediate communitarian capitalism that Etzioni believes exists. His account provides a realistic depiction of our everyday economic reality:

> Accordingly, *competition thrives not in impersonal, calculative systems* of independent actors unbound by social relations, as implied by the neoclassical paradigm, *nor in the socially tight world of communal* [tribal] *societies, but in the middle range,* where social bonds are strong enough to sustain mutual trust and low transaction costs but not so strong as to suppress exchange orientations.[12]

The neoclassical paradigm also tends to overlook the important role that cooperative behavior plays within a competitive market economy. Etzioni sees the realm of community as a third mediating space that lies between the state and the free market where "cooperation and values often find their support."[13] This is a basic communitarian insight. Moral values and moral decision-making do not take place in a social vacuum. They require the support of a community in which the individual is formed and which anchors the personality of the individual.

Etzioni points out that individuals who become isolated from all social ties can become physically ill and lose their mental balance and thus their ability to make rational choices, making them susceptible to the influence of crowds or demagogues.[14] This was the insight Drucker had concerning the communal character of fascism. It provided a felt sense of community, but one that was exclusive of freedom. As such, the fascist form of community was defective. Drucker's notion of the plant community was supposed to provide a social context within which persons could find meaningful social relationships that allow them to participate in directing their social lives, just as we participate in the direction of our political lives together within a democratic polity. According to Eileen Appelbaum, there has traditionally been a focus on the dynamics of small groups in work reform theories. In the tradition of American human relations theory there is a basic human need for cooperation. She cites Mayo on this basic dimension of human existence, "Every social group, at whatever level of culture, must face and clearly state two perpetual and recurrent problems of administration. It must secure for its individual and group membership: (1) The satisfaction of material and economic needs, and (2)

The maintenance of spontaneous cooperation throughout the organization."[15]

The neoclassical ideal-type of the lone individual is an undersocialized individual according to Etzioni's model. Here the group plays no role in shaping the attitudes of the individual. Indeed, the group is a sort of social fiction. Within his model, to isolate an individual in their work environment is to do them damage. "The administrator is dealing with well-knit human groups and not with a horde of individuals. Wherever it is characteristic . . . that these groups have little opportunity to form, the immediate symptom is turnover, absenteeism, and the like."[16] Mayo sought to turn the human need for cooperation to the benefit of organizations.

On the other hand, the person who is bound to the group without question, as in fascist societies, is an over-socialized individual. Here the group has a reality over and beyond the individual, shaping the individual's attitudes so as to maintain the solidarity of the group. The middle ground is represented by Etzioni's (and Drucker's) ideal of community. Here the individual has strong social ties but also plays an active role in shaping the community. There is thus a healthy tension between the individual and the group that allows persons to maintain their moral balance.

Deontology and the Plant Community

Amitai Etzioni's work, *The Moral Dimension*, has a distinctively deontological character. Indeed, Part I of his book is titled, "Beyond Pleasure: The Case for Deontological Social Sciences." A deontological ethical approach is one that focuses on the idea of duty. As we have seen, Etzioni argues that people often act for the sake of the rightness of their action. This is a basic deontological insight that Immanuel Kant described in terms of a good will. A good will is one that chooses to do what is right solely because it is right, based on an inner commitment (autonomy of the will) as opposed to a compulsion initiated by some external stimulus (heteronomy of the will).

Can such an ethical ideal have application in the business world? We have already seen the example of Aaron Feuerstein. Etzioni points out quite concretely that there are many instances of people who act unselfishly. A number of experiments have shown the extent of altruism within a given population. He cites experiments in which people return "lost" wallets and will take the time and effort to return money to an "Institute for Research in Medicine".[17] Within a business context, it is common for people to make investments at least partly out of a concern for social issues. There are green investments, for example, that take into account the environmental qualities of the goods and services provided by companies. The saving behavior of people can be understood as being partly a moral matter. Many people save because they believe it is wrong to be in debt and also because they believe they have a moral duty to do so for the sake of their children.[18] So, there is much evidence that people act altruistically and that their altruism extends into their business dealings.

Norman E. Bowie developed a remarkable study of business life from the perspective of a deontological ethic which provides a foundation in ethical theory for Etzioni's deontological approach in socio-economics. His study shows that Immanuel Kant's duty ethic has practical application to a wide range of issues in business life. Indeed, Bowie's book provides a thoroughgoing and coherent account of business life within a capitalist setting from the perspective of Kant's deontological ethical theory.[19] From this perspective, Bowie hoped to show that business firms can be both moral and profitable.

Bowie begins his study by showing that immoral business practices are self-defeating. This comports with Kant's insight that the moral law, or categorical imperative, is rational and universal in its application. According to Kant, the moral law is a moral standard that derives from human practical reason. Human beings, in Kant's view, are self-legislating beings, i.e., we are able to make our own law for ourselves. As such, human beings are able to make free choices inasmuch as freedom of the will involves making our own law for ourselves. This is what Kant called "Autonomy of the Will." If I can make my own law for myself and follow it, then I am a free being. Autonomy of the will can be understood in contrast with what Kant called "Heteronomy of the Will." This is a case in which the law I follow in making my choices is imposed on me from outside my will.

But is every law or maxim I make for myself also a moral law applying to all persons? It is commonly accepted that a moral law applies equally to all persons. If it is wrong for me to steal from you, it is likewise wrong for you to steal from me. All persons possess a moral equality in this way. Obviously, it is not the case that every law I might make for myself is also a moral law applying universally to all persons. Suppose I make it my law that I need not pay my debts. I have the freedom to make this my law. But is it also a moral law? How can I know if it is a moral law? Kant's approach is to take the law I make for myself and universalize it so that it applies to all persons. If the universalized law can be applied consistently in practice then it is rational and a moral law. Universalizing the law I made for myself would produce a law that no one must pay their debts. But what would be the practical outcome of a law that no one has to pay their debts? It seems that no one would ever give a loan. So the entire practice of lending would collapse. The practice of not paying our debts as a matter of principle would be self-defeating and is not rational. It is pragmatically self-contradictory. So that is not a moral law.

Generalizing on this approach, Kant formulated a general moral standard that requires we follow only those maxims, or moral rules, that can be universalized in the way we have described. "Act according to that maxim by which you can at the same time will that it should become a universal law."[20] This is one of three formulations of the moral law as construed by Kant that Bowie applies to determine how a business enterprise should be organized and what management principles would be appropriate if it were to follow Kant's moral theory.[21] The other two formulations are the Respect for Persons and Kingdom of Ends formulations. We will look at these later. For now, the first formulation, that of Universalizability, implies that I ought not to act according to a rule that exempts me from a practice that ought to apply to all others. So, it would not be rational to expect that all others ought to pay their debts but I need not.

Bowie goes on to cite other very interesting examples of business practices that are self-defeating in this way. Persons who make it a practice of writing bad checks can lead to the banning of the practice of cashing checks altogether. Bowie notes that on the East Coast it is uncommon to be able to cash a check while in the

Midwest it is a much more common practice.[22] The person who writes bad checks is following an irrational maxim or moral rule. They wish to exempt themselves from a practice that they would like all others to follow, namely, to always write checks that are covered. But if their own practice were made universal, or merely widespread, the entire practice collapses. It is self-defeating.

Bowie further notes that such irrational behavior is deleterious to business overall in that it leads to an increase in transaction costs. The greater the lack of trust, the greater the transaction costs involved. If people made it a general practice to not pay their bills, then economic transactions would become impossible.[23]

Another example along these same lines is one I have observed myself. In some parts of the city of St. Louis it is required that persons pre-pay for gasoline while in others it is not. The practice of not paying for gas after pumping it leads to the collapse of the practice altogether if it becomes universalized or merely wide-spread. The result is an increase in the inconvenience of pumping gas. From the perspective of Kant's ethical theory, the maxim to not pay for gas I have pumped is not rational because it is a self-defeating practice when made into a universal law.

In general, Kant argued that any practice that cannot be univer-salized consistently is immoral because it is irrational from a prac-tical point of view. The deontological character of Kant's ethical approach can be seen in the fact that Kant was not concerned with the consequences of our actions but with the rationality of our in-tentions. If I were able to get away with pumping gas without pay-ing or write a bad check without in fact collapsing the economy on any given occasion, those actions would not thereby be morally acceptable. As a matter of principle, they are morally impermissi-ble because the maxim (or rule) of my action is not rational. A person of good will refrains from doing things contrary to the moral law simply because it is contrary to the moral law. This may seem to be a curtailment of my freedom, but since the moral law is one I give myself (and which is universally valid at the same time), if I follow this law I am exercising my freedom.

Now, Bowie applies this standard for ethical decision making to a broad range of business practices. He believes that business is constituted of a number of standard practices and that Kant's un-derstanding of the moral law as a categorical imperative applies very well to business practices.[24] Perhaps the most significant area of application of Kant's categorical imperative in business lies in the area of contracts. According to Bowie's account, a contract at bottom is a promise. What would happen if people decided to make contracts with the intention of not keeping them? Kant's ethical principle can provide a ready answer. If we were to make it a universal law that contracts could be broken at will, then the practice of making contracts would break down. This law would be practically incoherent and thus self-defeating because no one would be willing to make any contracts.[25] The same line of reasoning applies to theft by managers, employees, or customers. If theft were made a universal practice, then private property would be impossible. But private property is a standard practice and so theft is self-defeating.[26] Likewise, coercive or deceptive practices could not be universalized without inconsistency.

In general, such practices undercut themselves when seen as universally accepted. In fact, Bowie points out that the possibility of common business exchanges breaks down long before a given practice, like not paying one's debts, becomes universal.

One way to think about the categorical imperative is in terms of the Golden Rule, "Do unto others as you would have others do unto you". I would not allow for a coercive or deceptive practice if I knew that such practices were to be universalized, and thus practiced against me. But beyond that, even if I were willing to accept such a devil's compact, the practices in question depend upon the person being coerced or deceived not having the power to avoid being coerced or knowing of the deception. In that case, the person who suffers from the coercion or deception **cannot** accept the practice. It therefore represents heteronomy of the will since it must be imposed on the person.[27]

On the other hand, we can note positively that when people generally act according to the universalizability criterion of the moral law, then business exchanges become possible. Bowie turns to the creation of the Russian stock exchange after the fall of the Soviet Union as an example here. According to his account, the Russian exchange had great difficulty getting off the ground because Russian companies tended to not give out accurate information to the public. As a result, no one would be willing to invest in them. But after some companies developed a reputation for truth-telling, investors were willing to invest in them.[28] This was the basis of the great danger surrounding the recent accounting scandal in the United States. If people lose confidence in the truthfulness of companies then they will no longer invest in them. The standard of truthfulness has thus been institutionalized in the role of the Securities and Exchange Commission in regulating businesses. There is, according to Bowie, a moral threshold that makes business practices possible.

Bowie provides other examples of businesses that have thrived partly because of their reputation for being honest. While it is true that a given company may have a competitive advantage by dealing dishonestly (at least for the short term) while all others are being honest, it is also true that a company may gain a competitive advantage for dealing honestly while all or most others deal dishonestly (or are perceived to be dishonest).[29] Remarkably, Bowie had himself found a car repairman who was in this enviable position. Leonard Swap uses Castle Rock Entertainment as an example of the same principle. It has a reputation for being open and honest in an industry in which those qualities are relatively rare. This has contributed to the company's success. "Having a reputation among talent agents for giving honest responses—quickly— means that the agents view Castle Rock as a good company to work with."[30]

Again, a Kantian ethic would say it is not because acting honestly augments the bottom line that we should do so. We should do so because it is the right thing to do. This is a stringent standard. But Etzioni has shown that such a concern for moral integrity is a real one for many people. Having said that, it is also true that acting honestly in business can contribute to the profitability of a company over the long term. The relationships businesses have with customers as well as those they maintain with their suppliers or other business alliances are crucial to their long-term profitability. Dishonest dealings, on the contrary, can lead to multibillion dollar losses, as in the case of GM and Volkswagen cited by Bowie. In this case, a GM employee who later moved to Volkswagen misappropriated proprietary information in order to reduce supplier costs. GM eventually sought $4 billion in damages and finally settled out of court. The cost to GM's reputation among suppliers added to the damage it suffered.[31]

Bowie closes the first chapter of his book with a reflection on the value of trust in business transactions. As he notes, "Management theorists have discovered trust."[32] Trust and trustworthiness underlie the possibility of business transactions both within and between firms. Without trust it can be seen that transaction costs would rise to a prohibitive level. As such, Bowie develops an argument that it is contrary to the moral law, the categorical imperative, to act in ways that undercut one's own trustworthiness. "Thus, to engage in activities that make one less trustworthy is to adopt a maxim that is pragmatically (volitionally) inconsistent."[33]

Respect for Persons

We noted above that Kant developed three formulations of the categorical imperative. He saw these as different expressions of the same moral law. The first formulation can be seen as prohibitive in the sense that it excludes maxims that cannot be universalized without contradiction, either conceptual or pragmatic. Kant's second formulation of the moral law is more positive and outlines how we ought to treat all persons. "Act so that you treat humanity, whether in your own person or in that of another, always as an end, and never as a means only."[34] The essential idea here is to treat all persons with respect. Kant held that all persons have an infinite worth that he called dignity. The dignity of persons is inherent and therefore cannot be lost. In this way it is analogous to the idea of an inalienable right. It cannot be separated from the person. To treat persons with respect is to recognize their human dignity. This idea can be seen as underlying Drucker's notion of status. Persons can be said to have status because they have the dignity of a person and are therefore members of a moral community.

According to Kant, the dignity of persons is grounded in their freedom to choose their own ends. We have already mentioned the idea of autonomy of the will. A person is a free being, in Kant's view, because persons have the ability to make their own law for themselves. This is equivalent to being able to choose one's own ends (or goals). The second formulation of the moral law asserts that we have a moral duty to respect this freedom of persons. Strictly speaking, we have a moral obligation to respect the rational goals of persons. If I were to choose to sell myself into slavery, that would not be a rational goal because it would undermine my own freedom. We might say that it would be a free choice that is incompatible with my own human dignity, reducing myself to a mere means, and making it impossible to make further free decisions. In other words, we can abuse our freedom. However, such an abuse of freedom can be avoided if we understand what it means to be free in terms of the ability to make universal laws. And such laws are also moral laws.

Now, persons are said to be "ends-in-themselves" because they are able to freely establish their own ends. In contrast to persons, objects can be used as a means of achieving our goals. In saying that we should never treat persons as a means only, the second formulation of Kant's categorical imperative asserts that we ought not to treat persons like objects. But it is important to note that the moral law forbids treating persons as a means ONLY. As such, it is permissible to treat persons as a means, as long as we also treat them as ends-in-themselves, i.e., as free beings. Economic transactions would be impossible if we could never treat persons as a means to achieving our goals. But at the same time, we have a moral obligation to never treat persons as a mere means. We must always treat them with respect.

How would the application of this formulation of the moral law to our business practices shape them? Chapter two of Bowie's work on business ethics applies the idea of respect for persons to the relationship between employers and their employees. However, it is obvious that the principle applies equally well to the entire range of stakeholders of a business firm.

At a minimum, the idea of respect for persons excludes deceptive and coercive treatment of employees. This seems obvious. Deception and coercion bypass the assent of persons that is essential to them as rational self-governing beings. But the respect for persons principle also implies that persons ought not to be treated as just another capital asset of a business firm along with other resources. From this perspective the term that is commonly used in personnel departments, "human capital", is problematic. Here Bowie brings up the issue of equal proportional marginal productivity. Like many ideas in management theory, it sounds a lot more difficult than it really is. According to this approach, if the cost of machines is higher than that of labor, then machines should be cut and labor increased. But if the cost of labor is higher than that of machines, then labor should be cut and the use of machines should be increased.[35]

Of course, in those industries that can be automated the usual substitution that is made is machines for labor. Peter Drucker pointed to the human consequences of such a decision. It undermines the status of workers, their membership in a community. From a moral perspective, the substitution is not equivalent because the dignity of persons is not equivalent to the price of a machine. The usual practice of downsizing for the sake of cutting costs is not compatible with the dignity of persons.[36]

Bowie thus argues that massive layoffs are not compatible with the moral requirement to treat all persons with respect. The threat of arbitrary lay-offs may be seen as coercion, forcing employees to accept contract terms they would otherwise not accept. It is not an explicit component of contracts between employers and their employees.[37] It would seem that at this point a moral requirement has come into direct conflict with an economic necessity. This would be true if there were no alternatives to layoffs as a means of cost-saving. But there are simple alternatives that do not involve treating employees as a mere means of saving costs like an across the board pay cut, cutting the work week, early retirement, and retraining.[38]

Such alternatives would seem to be morally preferable in that they promote and maintain a sense of community among the firm's internal constituents as they share both benefits and burdens. It seems highly preferable to laying off large numbers of persons as a cost-cutting measure in order to raise the price of the company's stock, and perhaps the compensation package of the company's chief executive. The NuCor Corporation employed just such an alternative during the '83-'84 recession. They put all employees on a 2-3 day work week. This included the CEO of the company. Of course, when the company was able to restore the workers to a full work week, their morale and productivity were very high. The sense of sharing burdens builds a strong bond that is typical of a community.[39]

This is an example of what Heilbroner alluded to at the beginning of this chapter. To lay off massive numbers of people during an economic downturn seems to be an economic necessity. But the fact that there are alternatives to such a policy places a moral burden on business leaders who must decide which of the social possibilities before them to actualize. Heilbroner's point was that within a society of abundance we have the possibility of transcending economic necessity and of making choices based on other social goals which could have the effect of humanizing our economic lives. Thus, a non-economic goal that might direct our economic choices is to maintain the community ties that form the foundation of our economic and social lives together.

What is significant for the purposes of our study is that there is a shared sense of community within such a firm. It is interesting to note that there are existing firms that have a strong community structure and the effect on productivity is generally quite positive. Bowie actually lists eighteen companies from the Fortune 100 best companies that have no-layoff policies.[40] One of the best companies that we can cite in this regard is IDEO. It was featured in *BusinessWeek* for its culture of innovation.[41] Its co-founder, David Kelly, has remarked that if their employees are constantly worried about being fired it cannot contribute to their creativity and productivity.[42] Instead, he sees his firm as promoting a more nurturing environment where people can develop their skills. This is an enlightened view, especially in a "knowledge economy" where the skills of workers are the most important asset of a company. But it also conforms to the second formulation of Kant's categorical imperative to treat all persons with respect.

Twenty-five years ago Lester Thurow described a system of remuneration based on bonuses that obviates the use of employees as a mere means of cost-cutting and would contribute to a sense of community within firms. Rather than laying-off large numbers of employees during a time of recession, say, and thus lowering their income to zero, bonuses could be paid out as a significant part of a pay package. The level of the bonuses could be tied to the company's value-added. This would give employees periodic feedback on their productivity. As the productivity of the firm rises, the bonuses of all employees rise. And as the firm's productivity falls, the bonuses of all employees fall. During a recession the income of all employees would fall, but it would not drop to zero for any of them (unless the firm goes out of business altogether). Thurow points out this would have a positive macro-economic effect. If many people lose their income through layoffs they lose their purchasing power, thus deepening a recession. There is also a cost to the public in providing unemployment benefits. The bonus method of remuneration, on the contrary, can have the effect of softening recessions. And, during such a downturn, firms can retool and their employees can be retrained. If people are laid off and later brought back when the economy rebounds, they tend to lose their skills.[43] According to William Ouchi,

> Twice in recent times, Hewlett-Packard has adopted the nine-day fort-night along with a hiring freeze, a travel freeze, and the elimination of perquisites. Each time these steps kept employees on while other companies in the industry had layoffs. The result at Hewlett-Packard has been the lowest voluntary turnover rate, the most experienced workforce in the industry, and one of the highest rates of growth and profitability.[44]

According to Appelbaum and Batt, some employers prefer this kind of variable pay for several reasons. In addition to increasing the flexibility of the firm, it can create an internal market within an organization which provides for a sense of buy-in for the employees since they have to share the risks associated with the enterprise as well as the benefits.[45]

Bowie takes up the issue of profit-sharing as a practice that is implied by the principle of respect for persons. One form of profit-sharing that is of particular interest in this regard is ESOPs or Employee Stock Ownership Plans. Such programs have the effect of enfranchising employees who now, of course, are also owners. Starbucks has extended stock ownership to its part-time employees.[46] This has contributed to employee loyalty which has resulted in a high retention rate. Employees have even contributed to the profitability of the company by creating new products. This is precisely what is supposed to happen in a knowledge economy. But workers that are enfranchised have a greater incentive to innovate. The policy of sharing both the risks and the rewards of economic activity within a firm is a good sign of a community structure.[47] Bowie describes several innovative profit-sharing plans including those employed at Intel and H. B. Fuller. Such plans are most effective in creating a sense of community in a firm when they are available to all of the employees and not just the top executives. It is interesting to note that ESOPs are sometimes employed as a last resort to save a failing company. However, it is not just the sharing of ownership but the sharing of responsibility that saves the business. This was part of the meaning of Drucker's assertion that today community must be based on the responsibility of its members.

Sharing risks and benefits can be essential to the innovation required to save companies that are threatened with closure. The Pratt and Whitney plant in Maine faced just this prospect. When the plant manager introduced a profit-sharing plan and required the workers to retrain, it did not seem to have the desired effect. This is because the workers did not have a sense of buy-in to the changes. After a system of democratic representation was initiated, the workers themselves developed a new pay scheme with new job classifications that rewarded workers for learning new methods and the plant was saved.[48] Where workers are also owners it would make sense for workers to participate in the decision-making process. We are fast approaching Drucker's notion of the plant community. But the notion of participatory management fits under Kant's third formulation of the moral law, the Kingdom of Ends formulation. Before we leave the respect for persons formulation, however, Bowie considers two other practices that are implied by the ideal of Respect for Persons, i.e., open book management and the provision of meaningful work.

Open book management is valuable since employers and employees typically meet in the market having unequal positions, in part due to the fact that management has information labor does not. This gives management a decisive advantage over labor in contract negotiations. It also provides an opportunity for deception on the part of management. So, open book management is supposed to eliminate this opportunity for deception. Bowie notes that it is a technique that has been applied successfully by a number of companies including Intel, Allstate, and Herman Miller. For persons to act as autonomous decision makers, they must have adequate information.[49] It is also necessary to facilitate the interaction and discretionary action required for innovation in the setting of an information economy. In open book management, employees are provided with all of the financial information of the company.

They are also enfranchised with a profit-sharing plan based on the overall profits of the company. This can have the effect of eliminating the need for multiple layers of supervision as employees are led to make responsible decisions on their own initiative.[50] What is of special interest here is that social arrangements that are morally sound also result in a high degree of utility from a business perspective. It could be argued that such a conjunction of positive features is Pareto optimal i.e., the best of all possible worlds, or at least the best of which we are capable.

In his depiction of knowledge creation in Japanese firms, Ikujiro Nonaka argues that redundancy is essential to the diffusion of knowledge within an organization. In this context he notes,

> Free access to company information also helps build redundancy. When information differentials exist, members of an organization can no longer interact on equal terms, which hinders the search for different interpretations of new knowledge. Thus Kao's top management does not allow any discrimination in access to information among employees. All company information (with the exception of personnel data) is stored in a single integrated database, open to any employee regardless of position.[51]

In addition to open book management, Bowie prescribes the provision of meaningful work as being implied by Kant's principle of respect for persons. This follows because the categorical imperative implies that we pursue our own perfection and the happiness of others. Bowie sets out six principles of meaningful work that fit the requirements of Kant's principle of respect for persons.[52] They support the autonomy of workers by providing both the financial and social support necessary to be self-legislating. Of course, this assumes that it is possible to provide these things. An old ethical rule of thumb is "ought implies can". If the economy were to reach equilibrium below the level where it is possible to provide a living wage[53], then it cannot be morally obligatory to do so.

But what can be seen is that the moral requirement for meaningful work makes perfect economic and management sense in an information economy. It may not be the case, as Drucker suggested, that the interests of the firm and those of the workers are incompatible with each other. For the social benefits that Drucker depicted in terms of the status of the worker can contribute in the end to their productivity. This is precisely how Velasquez approaches the problem of overspecialization of tasks that is associated with the so-called "rational organization" model of the firm. The traditional model of the organization that is epitomized in the automobile production line seeks to maximize efficiency by specializing tasks along two axes, a horizontal axis and a vertical axis. The horizontal axis includes the restriction of the range of tasks performed for a given job and increasing the repetition of those tasks. Vertical specialization involves the restriction of control and decision-making surrounding the task in terms of the pace of work, its organization, etc.[54] Velasquez cites an auto assembly-line worker who described his work day for Studs Terkel's book, *Working: People Talk About What They Do All Day and How They Feel About What They Do.*

> I start the automobile, the first welds. . . . The welding gun's got a square handle, with a button on the top for high voltage and a button on the bottom for low. . . . We do about thirty-two jobs per car, per unit. Forty-eight units an hour, eight hours a day. Thirty-two times forty-eight times eight. Figure it out. That's how many times I push that button. . . . It don't stop. It just goes and goes and goes. . . . I don't like the pressure, the intimidation. How would you like to go up to someone and say, "I would like to go to the bathroom?" If the foreman doesn't like you, he'll make you hold it, just ignore you. . . . Oh, yeah, the foreman's got somebody knuckling down on him, putting the screws to him. But a foreman is still free to go to the bathroom, go get a cup of coffee. He doesn't face the penalties. . . .[55]

This example is a good illustration of both horizontal and vertical specialization. The tasks are highly repetitive and the worker has no control over the conditions of his work. It is easy to see that this mode of organization of work does not satisfy the conditions for meaningful work outlined by Bowie. The long-term result of this method of organizing work is a high level of worker dissatisfaction which can increase the ill health effects of their work, leading to lost work hours.[56] So, this approach does not really increase efficiency in the long run.

Velasquez provides guidelines for overcoming the deleterious effects of overspecialization. They involve providing just the very conditions for meaningful work that we have seen are also demanded from a moral perspective. Velasquez points to a number of research findings that suggest experienced meaningfulness, experienced responsibility, and knowledge of the results of their productive efforts contributes to greater job satisfaction for workers.[57] If a job is "broadened horizontally" the employee has a wider variety of tasks. If a job is "deepened vertically" the employee has greater control over the tasks she or he performs in terms of the speed of the work, the persons with whom the task is performed, the break times, etc.[58] A famous comic example in this regard is the chocolate factory line skit that Lucile Ball did many years ago on the *I Love Lucy* show. Her character found herself working on a chocolate production line that unexpectedly begins to move much more quickly. Lucy must cope with the increase in the speed of the production line as best she can. But who decided the line should speed up? It was not those doing the job. And how did that affect their morale? On the other hand, Appelbaum and Batt give an example of workers whose tasks are both horizontally broad, and vertically deep. They note that the workers at the ceramics plant in Corning, New York, work in self-managing teams. They participated in the design of the plant, applying their intimate knowledge of the productive process. There is extensive communication across the organization and the workers are given information about the organization's business position. Again, the degree of buy-in by the workers is significant. In fact, the workers developed their own system of remuneration based on skill levels they determined for themselves. Finally, the workers at the plant have a role in the hiring process and the on-going training at the plant.[59]

Bowie goes on to argue that the provision of meaningful work can add a competitive advantage. It is an idea that has made its way into contemporary management theory, (See Jeffrey Pfeffer's *Competitive Advantage through People*), and there are examples of successful companies that put it into practice. Pfeffer's 16 points for successful management are supportive of Kant's ideal of respect for persons.[60]

Bowie quotes Max DePree, the CEO of Miller Furniture, at length as perhaps the best example of a Kantian approach to work as a function of respect for the dignity of the worker. It is worth repeating here:

For many of us who work there exists an exasperating discontinuity between how we see ourselves as persons and how we see ourselves as workers. We need to eliminate the sense of discontinuity and to restore a sense of coherence in our lives. . . . Work should be and can be productive and rewarding, meaningful and maturing, enriching and fulfilling, healing and joyful. Work is one of the greatest privileges. Work can even be poetic.

What is it most of us really want from work?. . . We would like a work process and relationships that meet our personal needs for belonging, for contributing, for meaningful work, for the opportunity to make a commitment, for the opportunity to grow and be at least reasonably in control of our own destinies.[61]

Our position is that the coherence DePree is looking for in the workplace is possible within a social context that is characterized by a sense of community. Community is a social arrangement that recognizes the social needs of workers, as Drucker pointed out, and also recognizes the moral significance of the freedom of persons.

The Kingdom of Ends

Kant's third formulation of the moral law is known as the Kingdom of Ends formulation. According to Kant, "Every rational being must act as if he, by his maxims, were at all times a legislative member in the universal realm of ends."[62] The idea of a kingdom of ends is essentially that of a moral community. And thus, the third chapter of Bowie's book on *Business Ethics* is "The Firm as a Moral Community." In this chapter Bowie asks, "what would the business firm as a Kantian moral community look like?"[63] Since we are not alone in our freedom, Kant held that we ought to pursue freely chosen ends that are compatible with the freely chosen ends of all other persons. He held that the shared purposes of persons ought to be compatible with each other to the degree that they are rational purposes.

In a business context, this version of the categorical imperative underlines the degree to which our economic lives require cooperation as well as competition. This is widely recognized today in the formation of work teams. In a sense, an entire organization is a work team. In this regard, Etzioni referred to the "Morality of Cooperation".[64] He notes that cooperation is extensive within a market economy within and between firms and between the market and the government. Bowie contrasts problem-solving teams with quality circles and relates them both to the productivity of an organization and its character as a moral community. In the context of the problem-solving approach, the number of contacts between workers is wider than in that of quality circles, which requires a greater degree of trust within the organization. And this contributes to forming a moral community within the organization.[65] IDEO is a firm that employs such problem-solving teams and allows the workers to form such teams themselves rather than imposing the membership of the teams from above.[66]

Bowie finds that Douglas McGregor's work, *The Human Side of Enterprise*, supports Kant's Kingdom of Ends formulation of the categorical imperative. Whereas the Theory X form of management assumes that persons are not trustworthy and therefore require constant monitoring to insure that they are pursuing the goals of the firm, a Theory Y approach sees persons as able and willing to be self-monitoring based on a commitment to responsible self-direction.[67]

McGregor's theory Y approach builds trust and confidence among the members of a firm as well as a sense of community. By contrast, Bowie points out how the use of surveillance techniques has grown in firms.[68] This is an expression of a Theory X approach which sees individuals as rapacious and untrustworthy. Of course, the use of such devices represents a cost of doing business and may have the effect of reducing productivity because it tends to undermine the creative initiative of employees. It also undermines a sense of community in firms and may violate the rights of employees to privacy. In the end, it may also be a self-fulfilling prophecy of a sort because the general culture of the firm is one that expects people to behave in an untrustworthy way.

Manuel Velasquez takes up the issue of the rights of employees in his treatment of the "Political Organization" model of the firm. He notes that there may be circumstances in which the use of surveillance techniques like cameras, listening devices, and computer monitoring is justified. But he argues that such techniques ought to be balanced against the rights of employees.[69] Within the political organization model of the firm, employees are seen as being citizens of the firm having rights that limit the power of the firm to interfere in their lives, just as the power of the state is limited by the rights of citizens of the state.

> Janice Bone was a payroll clerk for Ford Meter Box, a small manufacturer in Wabash, Indiana. Ford Meter Box prohibited its employees from smoking and conducted urine tests to verify compliance. [Not just smoking on the job.]
>   Nicotine traces showed up in Bone's urinalysis and she was fired. Bone filed suit and the Indiana legislature passed a statute protecting workers who smoke outside the workplace from termination. . . . Senator Carl Franklin, a supporter of Oklahoma's Off-The-Job Smoking Protection statute says, 'When they start telling you [that] you can't smoke on your own time, the next thing you know they'll tell you [that] you can't have sex but once a week, and if you have sex more than once a week, you're fired' . . . The ACLU fears that the list of prohibitions will expand, as with U-Hall, to include weight, drinking, or as in Athens, Georgia—cholesterol-level tests for all city job applicants.[70]

We noted in the first chapter that it has been widely recognized that the structure of authority in business firms is analogous to the structure of authority in the modern state. Velasquez characterizes a state as being,

> a) a centralized decision-making body of officials who b) have the power and recognized authority to enforce their decisions on subordinates (citizens); these officials c) make decisions that determine the public distribution of social resources, benefits, burdens among their subordinates, and d) they have a monopoly on the power to which their subordinates are subject.[71]

The analogy that obtains between this kind of social structure and that of business firms is striking. For, managers have these same sorts of powers over their employees.[72] The recognition of the political dimension of modern business firms is a signal achievement of modern management theory. In fact, there is evidence that people like John Locke may have modeled the modern state on business firms.[73]

But there are different kinds of states having different sources of legitimacy. In chapter two we noted that the question of the legitimacy of the (political) authority of managers was one that Berle and Means took up in *The Modern Corporation and Private Prop-*

erty (1932). States differ not only in their political legitimacy but also in their moral legitimacy. Drucker studied fascist states and noted that they depend on the use of slave labor. Workers in the democracies, on the other hand, were recognized as have status. We could say they have the dignity of persons. From the perspective of Drucker's study, we might ask whether we fought the Second World War so that people living in democratic societies could work for firms that resemble fascist states, i.e., firms that treat their workers as a mere means of production or as industrial slaves. Here are several examples,

> ●After the Homestead strike in the Carnegie mills (put down by the dispatch of 8000 militia [in 1892]) . . . . [Henry] Frick imposed a twelve-hour day seven days per week, with a twenty-four-hour stretch every two weeks; abolished all grievance committees; kept all wage scales secret; eliminated extra pay for Sunday work; forbade all workers' meetings; and cut wages far below prestrike levels.[74]

● "An angry judge told lawyers for Microsoft Corp. to urge their boss to reconsider new language in contracts for temporary workers that would waive their right to court-ordered additional pay or benefits"[75]

> ●A leading labor rights activist accused major U.S. retailing companies Wal-Mart, Kmart, and J.C. Penney of sub-contracting in a Nicaraguan "sweatshop" despite efforts to end exploitation of Central American, Caribbean and Asian workers.
>
> Charles Kernaghan, who 18 months ago exposed a factory in Honduras that made clothes for Wal-Mart carrying the name of American TV personality Kathie Lee Gifford, told reporters Tuesday an investigation found sewers making 15 cents an hour and children as young as 15 in one apparel plant.[76]

● "A coalition of sporting goods manufacturers, child welfare advocates and labor groups on Friday announced a plan to end the use of child labor in making hand-stitched soccer balls in Pakistan."[77]

The notion of status developed by Drucker has a sociological and moral meaning with political implications. If business firms are modeled on democratic states, then it can be argued that persons working for a business firm ought to have rights in the economic order that are analogous to the rights we recognize in the political order. Among the economic rights Velasquez considers are the right to privacy, freedom of conscience, and the right to participate in the governance of the firm.[78] A democratic political organization satisfies the Kingdom of Ends formulation of the moral law in that it recognizes that the freedom and dignity of persons requires that they have the status of being both ruler and ruled. Thus, every member of an organization ought to have a voice in establishing the rules that will govern the group.[79] In an interview, Robert Hitt pointed out that the managers at the BMW plant in Spartanburg, South Carolina are careful in making rules since they will be applied to them as well.[80] The managers are not able to exempt themselves from the rules they make. In other words, the rules must be universalizable. Such rules tend to treat persons with respect.[81] An organization or social body that incorporates this kind of rule-making process is a kingdom of ends.

Bowie proposes seven principles for the organization of business firms that are consistent with the idea of a kingdom of ends.

1) The firm should consider the interests of all the affected stakeholders in any decision it makes.

2) The firm should have those affected by the firm's rules and policies participate in the determination of those rules and policies before they are implemented.

3) It should not be the case that for all decisions, the interests of one stakeholder take priority.

4) When a situation arises where it appears that the humanity of one set of stakeholders must be sacrificed for the humanity of another set of stakeholders, that decision cannot be made on the grounds that there is a greater number of stakeholders in one group than in another.

5) No principle can be adopted which is inconsistent [with the first formulation of the categorical imperative], nor can it violate the humanity in the person of any stakeholder in the sense of [the respect for persons formulation].

6) Every profit-making firm has an imperfect duty of beneficence. [An imperfect duty is one that we need to fulfill on some but not all occasions whereas a perfect duty is one we need to always fulfill. See p. 26 in Bowie]

7) Each business firm must establish procedures designed to insure that relations among stakeholders are governed by rules of justice.

These rules of justice are to be developed in accordance with principles 1-6 and must receive the endorsement of all stakeholders. They must be principles that can be publicly accepted and thus be objective in a Kantian sense.[82]

Bowie relates these principles to both management theory and actual businesses that exemplify them. So, they are not merely theoretical, but real-world principles. It is important to note that there is a variety of ways that these principles could be applied. If these principles imply the democratization of the workplace, there are various arrangements that will fulfill them to a greater or lesser degree, from direct democracy to indirect democracy, from a consultative to a participative approach. Velasquez provides a survey of the various forms of participatory management in his work on business ethics.[83] In addition to McGregor's distinction between theory X and Theory Y management approaches, Velasquez considers Raymond Miles' depiction of 1) the Traditional model 2) the Human Relations model and 3) the Human Resources model of management. Finally, he refers to Renis Likert's four systems of organization. They include, 1) the Exploitive Authoritarian, 2) the Benevolent Authoritarian, 3) the Consultative and 4) the Participative.[84]

The first two of these are not consistent with Kant's ethical theory because they fail to recognize persons as ends-in-themselves, i.e., having the freedom to choose their own ends. Participation in the decision-making process is a keynote of a Kantian approach to business ethics. While it may actually contribute to the overall efficiency of the firm by raising worker satisfaction, at a deeper level participation represents recognition of the dignity of persons.[85]

But the fact that participation in the decision-making process can add to productivity is not to be ignored either. Bowie shows that the characteristics of a participatory form of organization are also those of meaningful work.[86] This indicates that Kant was correct in seeing the different versions of the categorical imperative as being different formulations of the same moral law. They all contribute to the dignity of persons and thus promote the status of workers. So, the implications of one, the respect for persons formula, focus on the value of meaningful work, while the implications of the other, the kingdom of ends formula, focus on the value of participation in the decision-making process.

It is important to note that the elimination of authoritarian modes of organization does not entail the elimination of all hierarchy in the organization of business firms. A hierarchical structure need not be authoritarian. But again, Bowie makes the interesting observation that many businesses have begun to eliminate layers of hierarchy in their organizational structure.[87] This is usually done to improve the bottom line. It is also consistent with the needs of an information economy where the skills and knowledge of workers are recognized as the most important asset of a firm. Thomas A. Stewart describes how Levi Strauss allowed its fork lift truck drivers to become involved in the purchase of new trucks. He observes that the workers were able to purchase trucks that were more appropriate to the task and saved the company considerable money in the process.[88] But it also comports with the moral requirement to allow all of the members of an organization the ability to express their freedom as a member of the moral community. As we shall see when we take up the model of the circular organization in the next chapter, it is possible to achieve a non-authoritarian organizational structure without eliminating layers of management.

Participative organizations have multiple secondary beneficial effects like lowering absenteeism and reducing waste, and most importantly, increasing the interaction of the members of the organization.[89] In their study, *The New American Workplace*, Eileen Appelbaum and Rosemary Batt provide some evidence that positive results have been produced at Xerox and Corning after adopting a high performance team production model. Both of these organizations experienced productivity growth and a reduction in waste and product defects.[90] Thus, the moral demand for participation is consistent with the economic demand in capitalistic societies for efficiency and productivity. The traditional authoritarian hierarchical organization aims at these positive results but in the end produces several secondary ill effects like absenteeism and work slowdowns.[91] Management theory and ethical theory agree that it is not possible to separate the economic lives of persons from their humanity. According to Velasquez, the scope of participation in the workplace extends to "working hours, rest periods, organization of work tasks, and scope of responsibility of workers and supervisors."[92]

Recognizing the autonomy of workers can clearly affect retention as well. According to Mark Levin, CEO of Millennium Pharmaceuticals in Cambridge, Massachusetts, "If you hire outstanding people, you have to give them authority."[93] David Witte, CEO of the executive search firm Ward Howell International, suggests that freedom and responsibility are the best golden handcuffs. "I can easily take people from bureaucratic companies like Amoco or Exxon, but there's no way in hell I can steal from Joe Foster [who was the first to introduce self-managing teams at Tenneco Oil]."[94]

In addition to participation, we can cite consent as a marker of an organization that is consistent with Kantian moral requirements. According to Bowie, the requirement to obtain the consent of those affected by the rules of a firm indicates that a mere consultative approach is not adequate. Just as I ought not to make a decision to become a slave, the employment contract cannot be viewed as an agreement to give up my ability to be self-governing. Appelbaum and Batt tie this issue to economic performance. They note that the form and content of the participation are key to increasing performance, as well as some type of profit sharing scheme and the recognition of individual rights within the firm.[95]

Overall, Bowie believes that the Kantian moral requirement to recognize the autonomy of all persons leads to the conclusion that the workplace should be democratized. He calls for the establishment of some form of representation of all stakeholder groups in business organizations so they can consent to the rules of the organization. He suggests that some of the layers of management be replaced by teams that could participate in decision making. This would make of the firm a cooperative undertaking.[96] This is one approach to the democratization of the workplace that is possible. As we shall see shortly, there is another way to organize firms along democratic lines that need not flatten out the organization as Bowie suggests. For now, it should be observed that a flattening of the hierarchy of business firms may contribute to its overall efficiency. It is an approach that is consistent with contemporary management theory, especially in the age of the information economy. William Ouchi's Theory Z supports the democratization of the workplace, which comports perfectly with the requirements of

Kant's moral theory.[97] We can sum up these developments by observing that the conjunction of capitalism and community is the common endpoint of both moral reflection and management theory.

Bowie's application of Kant's ethical theory to the organization of the modern corporation presents a challenge to firms that have maintained the old rational organization model. He argues that the ethical ideal of treating all persons with respect implies a thoroughgoing democratization of the workplace. Persons who have freedom to choose their own ends or goals must have the ability to be self-governing. This applies to the workplace as much as it applies to the polis. When we recognize the capacity for the freedom of persons we are led to the demand for the formation of a moral community. Membership in this community is what Drucker called status. And it is remarkable that the economic demands of the modern information economy conform to the ethical demand to form a moral community. For, the kinds of innovations associated with democratization of the workplace also contribute to productivity by fostering innovation and work satisfaction. As Bowie has pointed out, people within business firms have a desire to be treated the way Kant's ethical theory proposes they ought to be treated.[98] In the next chapter we will see a proposal for a democratic corporation that is able to overcome the structural barriers that Drucker encountered in his attempt to unite the status and function of workers.

NOTES

1. Robert Heilbroner, *The Making of Economic Society*, 2ⁿᵈ ed., Prentice-Hall Inc., 1968, p. 221, (emphasis in the original).
2. Ibid., pp. 221,223.
3. See "Amartya Sen", Michael McPherson, in *New Horizons in Economic Thought: Appraisals of Leading Economists*, ed., Warren J. Samuels, Edward, Elgar Publishing Company, 1992, p. 294, "Most of our profession has opted whole-heartedly, and often naively, for simplification in the underlying behavioral and moral assumption."
4. Amitai Etzioni, *The Moral Dimension*, The Free Press, 1988, p. xi.
5. Ibid., p. 55.
6. Robert Heilbroner, "Controlling the Corporation", *In the Name of Profit*, Doubleday & Company, Inc., 1972, p. 238.
7. Norman E. Bowie, *Business Ethics: A Kantian Perspective*, Blackwell Publishers, 1999, p. 127.
8. Amitai Etzioni, *The Moral Dimension*, p. 208.
9. Quoted in Bowie, p. 139, from Dana Milbank, "Hiring Welfare People, Hotel Chain Finds, Is Tough But Rewarding," *Wall Street Journal* October 31, 1996, p. A1.
10. Edwin A. Murray Jr., "Ethics and Corporate Strategy", in *Corporations and the Common Good*, University of Notre Dame Press, 1986, p. 111.
11. Amitai Etzioni, *The Moral Dimension*, p. 211.
12. Ibid., (emphasis in the original). See George C. Lodge, "The Large Corporation and the New American Ideology, in *Corporations and the Common Good*, University of Notre Dame Press, 1986.
13. Amitai Etzioni, *The Moral Dimension*, p. 244.
14. Ibid., p. 9.
15. E. Mayo, *Social Problems of an Industrial Society*, Andover, MA: Andover Press, 1945, p. 9. Cited in *Manufacturing Advantage: Why High-Performance Work Systems Pay Off*, Eileen Appelbaum, Thomas Bailey, Peter Berg, Arne l. Kalleberg, Cornell University Press, 2000, p. 28.
16. Eileen Appelbaum, Thomas Bailey, Peter Berg, Arne l. Kalleberg, *Manufacturing Advantage: Why High-Performance Work Systems Pay Off*, Cornell University Press, 2000, p. 28.
17. Etzioni, Amitai, *The Moral Dimension*, p. 52. See Norman Bowie, "Challenging the Egoistic Paradigm", *Business Ethics Quarterly*, 1 (1991), pp. 1-21.
18. Ibid., p. 54.
19. See W. Evan and R. Freeman, "A Stakeholder Theory of the Modem Corporation: Kantian Capitalism," in T. Beauchamp and N. Bowie, *Ethical Theory and Business*, 4th edition (Englewood Cliffs, N. J.: Prentice Hall, 1993). For a critical account see Norman Barry, *Business Ethics* (London: Macmillan, 1998), chapter 4. A summary of Barry's view can be found at:

http://www.libertyhaven.com/theoreticalorphilosophicalissues/economics/freeen terpriseandentrepreneurship/stakeholder.shtml.

20. Immanuel Kant, *Foundations of the Metaphysics of Morals*. Translated by Lewis White Beck, (New York: Library of Liberal Arts, 1959), p. 39.

21. Norman E. Bowie, *Business Ethics: A Kantian Perspective*, Blackwell Publishers, 1999, p. 1.

22. Ibid., p. 12-13.

23. Ibid., p. 13.

24. Ibid., p. 15.

25. Ibid., p. 16.

26. Ibid.

27. See Christine M. Korsgaard, *Creating a Kingdom of Ends*, Cambridge University Press, 1996, p. 138-9.

28. Norman E. Bowie, *Business Ethics: A Kantian Perspective*, Blackwell Publishers, 1999, p. 20.

29. Ibid., p. 22.

30. Leonard Swap, *When Sparks Fly*, Harvard Business School Press, 1999, p. 104.

31. Norman E. Bowie, *Business Ethics: A Kantian Perspective*, Blackwell Publishers, 1999, p. 23.

32. Ibid., p. 30.

33. Ibid., p. 30.

34. Immanuel Kant, *Foundations of the Metaphysics of Morals*. Translated by Lewis White Beck, (New York: Library of Liberal Arts, 1959), p. 47.

35. Norman E. Bowie, *Business Ethics: A Kantian Perspective*, Blackwell Publishers, 1999, p. 42.

36. Ibid., p. 43.

37. Ibid., p. 49-50.

38. Ibid., p. 53.

39. Ibid., p. 56.

40. Ibid., p. 55.

41. *BusinessWeek*, May 17, 2004, pp. 86-94.

42. In an interview for an educational film, *The New Face of Work in America: Jobs Not What They Used to Be*. Films for the Humanities, 1996.

43. Lester C. Thurow, *The Zero-Sum Solution: Building a World-Class American Economy*, New York : Simon and Schuster, 1986, pp. 160-163. This method of remuneration was also described in *Slowth: The Changing Economy and How You Can Successfully Cope*, Martin Kupferman, Maurice D. Levi. New York: Wiley, c1980.

44. William Ouchi, *Theory Z*, pp. 118. Quoted in Bowie, p. 76.

45. Eileen Appelbaum and Rosemary Batt, *The New American Workplace*, ILR Press, an inprint of Cornell University Press, p. 80.

46. See "Starbucks and the Bean Stock", by Arlene Miller and Toby Copeland, http://www.fed.org/onlinemag/apr97/starb.html. See also, http://www.inc.com/magazine/19920701/4192.html

47. Norman E. Bowie, *Business Ethics: A Kantian Perspective*, Blackwell Publishers, 1999, p. 57.

48. Ibid., p. 107-8. Bowie cites Joseph B. White, "Dodging Doom: How a Creaky Factory Got Off the Hit List, Won Respect at Last," *Wall Street Journal* December 26, 1996, pp. A1-2.

49. Norman E. Bowie, *Business Ethics: A Kantian Perspective*, Blackwell Publishers, 1999, p. 54.

50. Bowie cites two sources, John Case, *Open Book Management*, New York: HarperCollins Publishers, 1995. See also, Jack Stack, *The Great Game of Business*, Currency, 1994.

51. Ikujiro Nonaka, "The Knowledge-Creating Company", Harvard Business Review on Knowledge Management, Peter F. Drucker, David Garvin, Leonard Dorothy, Straus Susan, John Seely Brown, Harvard Business School Press, 1998, p. 38

52. Norman E. Bowie, *Business Ethics: A Kantian Perspective*, Blackwell Publishers, 1999, p. 70-1.

53. See John K. Galbraith, *The American Economy*, New Brunswick, N.J., U.S.A.: Transaction Publishers, 1993. See Bowie, pp. 69-70.

54. Manuel Velasquez, *Business Ethics*, p. 460.

55. Ibid., p. 443.

56. See Robert Karasek and Töres Theorell, *Healthy Work: Stress, Productivity, and the Reconstruction of Working Life*, Basic Books, 1990.

57. Manuel Velasquez, *Business Ethics*, p. 462.

58. Ibid., p. 463.

59. Eileen Appelbaum and Rosemary Batt, *The New American Workplace*, ILR Press, New York, 1994, p. 87-8.

60. Norman E. Bowie, *Business Ethics: A Kantian Perspective*, Blackwell Publishers, 1999, p. 71, from Jeffrey Pfeffer, *Competitive Advantage Through People*, Chapter 2.

61. Norman E. Bowie, *Business Ethics: A Kantian Perspective*, Blackwell Publishers, 1999, p. 73., quoted from Max DePree, *Leadership Is An Art*, (New York: Dell Publishing, 1989), pp. 23, 32.

62. Immanuel Kant, *Foundations of the Metaphysics of Morals*. Translated by Lewis White Beck, (New York: Library of Liberal Arts, 1959), p. 57.

63. Norman E. Bowie, *Business Ethics: A Kantian Perspective*, Blackwell Publishers, 1999, p. 87.

64. Etzioni, *The Moral Dimension*, p. 243.

65. Norman E. Bowie, *Business Ethics: A Kantian Perspective*, Blackwell Publishers, 1999, p. 111.

66. For a depiction of this see, *The New Face of Work in America: Jobs Not What They Used to Be*. Films for the Humanities, 1996.

67. Douglass McGregor, *The Human Side of Enterprise*, p. 47-8. Quoted in Bowie, p. 85-6.

68. Norman E. Bowie, *Business Ethics: A Kantian Perspective*, Blackwell Publishers, 1999, p. 85.

69. Velasquez, p. 467-470

70. *Case Studies in Business Ethics*, Marianne Moody Jennings, West Publishing Company, p. 48.

71. Velasquez, pp. 465-466.

72. Velasquez, p. 466. Velasquez cites Earl Latham, "The Body Politic of the Corporation," in Edward S. Mason, ed., *The Corporation in Modern Society* Cambridge: Harvard University Press, 1960.

73. See "The Corporation and the Republic", Scott Buchanan, pp. 17-39, in *The Corporation Takeover*, edited by Andrew Hacker, Anchor Books, 1965.

74. Robert L. Heilbroner, et al., *In the Name of Profit*, Doubleday & Company Inc., 1972, p. 231-2.

75. http://www.abcnews.go.com/wire/US/AP19990114_631.html

76. http://www.yahoo.com/headlines/971112/news/stories/sweatshops_1.html

77. http://www.yahoo.com/headlines/970214/news/stories/soccer_1.html

78. Velasquez, pp. 463-484.

79. Norman E. Bowie, *Business Ethics: A Kantian Perspective*, Blackwell Publishers, 1999, p. 88.

80. *The New Face of Work in America: Jobs Not What They Used to Be.* Films for the Humanities, 1996.

81. Norman E. Bowie, *Business Ethics: A Kantian Perspective*, Blackwell Publishers, 1999, p. 88.

82. Ibid., pp. 90-1.

83. Velasquez, *Business Ethics*, 6th, pp. 380-382.

84. Ibid., pp. 476-7. See Raymond E. Miles, *Theories of Management: Implications for Organizational Behavior and Development*, McGraw-Hill, 1975, and Renis Likert, "From Production-and Employee-Centerdness to Systems 1-4", *Journal of Management*, vol. 5 (1979): 147-56.

85. Edmund L. Pincoffs, "Due Process, Fraternity, and a Kantian Injunction," in J. Roland Pennock and John W. Chapman (eds.) *Due Process*, Nomos XVIII New York: New York University Press, 1977, p. 179. Cited in Bowie, p. 92.

86. Norman E. Bowie, *Business Ethics: A Kantian Perspective*, Blackwell Publishers, 1999, p. 92.

87. Ibid., p. 98.

88. Thomas A. Stewart, "Why Leadership Matters," *Fortune* March 2, 1998, p. 82. Quoted in Bowie, p. 107.

89. Ibid., p. 100. Bowie cites, Renis Likert, *The Human Organization*, New York: McGraw-Hill, 1967.

90. Eileen Appelbaum and Rosemary Batt, *The New American Workplace*, ILR Press, New York, 1994, p. 145.

91. Norman E. Bowie, *Business Ethics: A Kantian Perspective*, Blackwell Publishers, 1999, p. 99. Bowie cites, Chris Argyris, *Integrating the Individual and the Organization*, New York: John Wiley & Sons, 1964.

92. Velasquez, p. 473.

93. Edward Prewitt, "What you Can Learn from Managers in Biotech", Management Update, 2 May 3. Quoted in *When Sparks Fly*, Leonard Swap, Harvard Business School Press, 1999, p. 184.

94. Leonard Swap, *When Sparks Fly*, p. 184.

95. Eileen Appelbaum and Rosemary Batt, *The New American Workplace*, ILR Press, New York, 1994, p. 21.

96. Norman E. Bowie, *Business Ethics: A Kantian Perspective*, Blackwell Publishers, 1999, p. 102.

97. Ibid., p. 104.

98. Ibid., p. 114.

Chapter IV
The Democratic Corporation

In 1994 Russell L. Ackoff published a study of business firms under the title, *The Democratic Corporation*. At that time, he saw business firms as undergoing a crisis associated with the rapid transformation of the economy. They were, in a sense, suffering from future shock. Of course, this is not the first time that institutions have had to undergo significant transformation. Ackoff depicts three distinct views of the firm that have held sway at different times in history. These include 1) The Mechanistic View, 2) The Organismic View, and 3) The Social System View. According to Ackoff, the first view of the firm derives from the eighteenth century view of the world developed by Isaac Newton. He saw the entire physical world as being a great clock-like mechanism. Business institutions were modeled on this view of the world at large. Accordingly, the workers were seen as replaceable parts of the mechanism. In other words, the relationships that obtained in such firms had the character of a machine. Human persons were treated as impersonal parts that could be used as a means of maximizing profit for the owner or owners. As long as workers were willing to follow the orders of their employer, they might be retained. If they were not willing to do so, they could easily be replaced. In this way, employers had the role of demi-gods who did not know about the personal concerns of their employees, and if they did know they would not care about them. The relationship of employer and employee was a wholly impersonal one, which was thought to contribute to the efficiency of the firm.[1]

As long as owners managed their own firms they retained control and the mechanistic view of the firm continued. But as firms became publicly held concerns, the management and ownership of firms became split. This resulted in a challenge to the legitimacy of the authority of the managers, who now tended to run the firm so as to maintain their authority. James Burnham showed this in his study, *The Managerial Revolution* (1941). In addition, unions began to press the claims of the workers over against management and the government placed limits on their activities. With the split between management and ownership, profit was no longer the end of the activity of the firm but rather served as a means of insuring its growth and survival. But, as Ackoff points out, the term "survival" is a biological term. The firm began to be seen as an organism. And this changes the relation of the parts of the organization to the whole.

It is interesting to note the way in which biological metaphors began to be applied to business firms. Ackoff points to such terms as the "head" of the firm as a biological metaphor. Businesses are said to be "viable", "healthy", or "sick".[2]

With respect to workers, Ackoff observes that with the advance of technology the skills of workers became of ever greater consequence to the growth and survival of firms. "As a result, they came to be treated more like difficult-to-replace organs than easily replaceable machine parts."[3] The health and safety of workers then began to take on a greater significance. But, Ackoff notes, the increased relevance of the function of workers did not immediately translate into an increased concern for their personal interests.[4] As workers began to lobby for better working conditions and experienced an increase in job security through their unions and social security, a tense opposition developed between management and labor. Ackoff likens the divide between management and labor in the organismic model of the firm to the old philosophical distinction between mind and body.[5] This is an apt analogy, since in the organismic model of the firm functions are strictly differentiated, just as the parts of an animal body are, and the mind is seen as supervening on the body.

According to Ackoff's account, the decline of the organismic view of an enterprise began with the Second World War. The workers who replaced the servicemen, i.e., "Rosie the Riveter", worked not primarily for the sake of profit but for patriotic reasons. This comports with Etzioni's claim that people act on the basis of diverse motives. Ackoff makes the interesting observation that during the war, managers essentially had to recognize the status of workers in order to achieve high levels of productivity.[6] That is to say, they had to treat them as human beings.

It is fascinating how the Second World War brought to the fore the issue of the status of the worker. Drucker saw it as the war unfolded and argued that this was the meaning of the struggle. It is equally astounding that the same American soldier who was praised for initiative in the war was told upon returning to civilian life that his place in the factory was such that "he does not direct but is directed." Ackoff provides penetrating insight into the new attitudes of workers after the war. They had experienced an authoritarian hierarchy in the military and tired of it. In addition, the more education and training they received, the more valuable they were to the firm. It only made economic sense to retain them longer since the investment of the firm in them was higher. It also made workers more mobile since they could take their skills elsewhere if their employer did not treat them well.[7]

Considered as a social system, it became necessary for managers to take into account the purposes and needs of the members of the system as well as others who interact with it. Ackoff considers this to be the basis for the stakeholder view of the firm.[8] This is perhaps the distinguishing characteristic of a social system over against a mechanism or an organism. For, a social system is composed of parts having purposes of their own that may diverge from the purposes of the organization.

> Social systems are systems that have purposes of their own, are made up of parts that have purposes of their own, and these larger containing systems include other systems that have purposes of their own. All these purposes came to be recognized as relevant to those who managed enterprises.[9]

Ackoff argues that just as the mechanistic conception of the organization was a reflection of the Industrial Revolution, the social systems conception of the organization is a reflection of what he designates the Second Industrial Revolution, the advent of the knowledge economy. His main point here is that systems have properties that machines do not. According to Ackoff, systems are characterized by five properties,

1) The whole has one or more defining functions.
2) Each part in the set can affect the behavior or properties of the whole.
3) There is a subset of parts that is sufficient in one or more environments for carrying out the defining function of the whole; each of these parts is separately necessary but insufficient for carrying out this defining function.
4) The way that the behavior or properties of each part of a system affects its behavior or properties depends on the behavior and properties of at least one other part of the system.
5) The effect of any subset of parts on the system as a whole depends on the behavior of at least one other subset.[10]

What this implies for the management of organizations is that, conceived as a system, the problem of the effective functioning of an organization is not a matter of supervising the individual actions of the members of the organization but the coordination of the many interactions of its members. And this represents a revolution in the problem of management. There are some interesting corollaries that follow from the structure of a system. First, "The defining function of a system cannot be carried out by any part of the system taken separately." And secondly, "when an essential part of a system is separated from the system of which it is a part, that part loses its ability to carry out its defining function."[11] As a result, it does not follow that the functioning of an organization will be improved by improving one of its parts. What is essential is the interaction of the part and the whole. Ackoff does a thought experiment that is instructive of this principle. He suggests that if we were to buy 555 different models of automobiles produced in the United States and tried to assemble a new car using the best parts from each car (the engine from the car having the best engine, the brake system from the car having the best brake system, etc.), we would not end up building the best car. "The performance of a system is not the sum of the performance of its parts taken separately, but the product of their interactions."[12]

The integration and coordination of the parts affects the operation of the whole and the whole also affects the operation of the parts. What Ackoff is looking for is a synergistic effect whereby the variety of behaviors of the parts of the system is increased. This kind of innovation and flexibility in the behaviors of the parts is what is missing in the mechanistic and organismic views of the organization. According to the systems model, the organization must contribute to the overall value of the parts. It is essential to realize that in this context, the morale of workers is key to the performance of the organization.[13]

Ackoff's treatment of the management of a business organization is abstract inasmuch as it considers human beings as being merely parts of a system. But it conforms very well to Bowie's approach which considered human beings as ends-in-themselves and the implications of that idea. The fact that a social system is made up of parts that have purposes, implies that the ability of persons to have purposes ought to be recognized and given its due, i.e., respected. Ackoff's social systems approach thus comports very well with Bowie's claim that workers like to be treated in the way Kant said they ought to be treated. The systems analysis applied by Ackoff suggests once again that the structural requirements of businesses as social systems overlap with the moral requirements of Kant's duty ethic. *"Participation, which is a form of self-determination, is itself a major source of satisfaction* and therefore of improved quality of life."[14]

Ackoff applies the social systems approach to the interactions of the divisions within an organization and to the interactions of an organization and the larger environment in which it exists. He notes that the acquisition of a new division that was profitable at the time of its acquisition may turn into a net loss for the acquiring company. This is an example of a part that does not function well in its interactions with the larger whole.[15] One result of the development of the social systems approach is that it makes the management of enterprises a much more subtle and complex affair.

In a mechanistic organization the value of the parts to the whole is determined by management. The subordinates at the lower levels of the organization are simply supposed to adjust their behavior to the whole. The whole need not adjust to the parts. It is interesting in light of Drucker's treatment of fascist economies and the development of the political organization model of business organizations we have seen, that Ackoff depicts such organizations as dictatorships. Ackoff goes on to note the loss of creativity in decision-making in such organizations. Mechanistic organizations lack flexibility and are thus not able to respond to a highly fluid environment.[16]

Within an organismic organization there is a limit on the range of choices available to its members. They are able to choose either the ends or the means they pursue, but not both. Usually the ends to be pursued are imposed from above and the workers are allowed to choose from a variety of means to attain their assigned ends. This allows for some flexibility in the organization. Ackoff notes that within an organization conceived as an organism the members of the group are able to respond and not merely react.[17] This strategy is characteristic of semiautonomous work groups and Management by Objectives. It is possible that within an organismically conceived organization the members are not allowed to choose the means to attain their ends. This approach involves the recognition of experts who are thought to be better equipped to know how certain ends can best be achieved.[18]

Evan though the organismically conceived organization is better able to adapt to change, Ackoff notes that its mode of adaptation is passive. It only responds to changes in the environment rather than actively initiating a change. An example of this is a case in which a business produces a product that is similar to one their competitor produces. This does not improve the company as a real innovation that a company initiates would.[19]

Another example is provided by Bernard Marcus, the cofounder of The Home Depot. He and Arthur Blank introduced a number of managerial innovations including what they called "The Stupid Hour". This involved the owners or other top managers meeting periodically with their workers so that the workers could bring out any practices that they considered to be stupid and that just make their lives miserable. Many of those practices would be eliminated in very short order. In an interview, Bernard Marcus noted that their competitors try to copy everything The Home Depot does. "They don't have an original idea in their brain."[20] In doing this, The Home Depot adapted actively while their competitors adapted passively. The Stupid Hour also gave The Home Depot employees a sense of ownership over their own jobs. It gave them a sense that they had status within the organization. The organismic enterprise cares about some of the interests of its members, like health and safety, but not the status of the workers. In this regard, Ackoff argues that managers should not try to impose improvements on workers but allow them to create their own work space environment since the workers know best what changes will raise the quality of their work experience.[21]

The enterprise that is viewed as a social system recognizes the purposes of all of its parts and the larger system within which it operates. According to Ackoff, it allows its members to participate in the choice of both the ends and means "that are relevant to them." This is perhaps the stumbling block that Drucker ran into. He thought that as workers it was not relevant to them to have a role in setting the ends of the enterprise. But, as we have seen, allowing persons to set their own ends comports very well with the ethical requirement of treating persons as ends-in-themselves. Ackoff notes that the social systems approach to the organization allows an organization's parts and the larger systems containing it to do what they could not otherwise do. The social systems approach can be seen as recognizing a wider sphere of relevance for workers and other stakeholders than Drucker would allow. Extending the choice of workers to both the means and the ends they pursue involves democratizing the workplace.[22]

Among the purposes of an enterprise conceived as a social system, according to Ackoff, is to produce and distribute wealth. But another important social function of the enterprise is to provide productive employment. This is why Ackoff points to alternatives to downsizing. It is not only the case that downsizing does not always work (failing to cut costs and lowering productivity by overburdening the remaining workers), but it fails to fulfill an essential social function of the firm. A significant example Ackoff provides here is that of a firm that was able to avoid bankruptcy by allowing its employees to buy out the transportation unit of the company based on a loan backed by the money the company could have directed to simply fire the employees of that unit. By outsourcing this unit, the company was able to avoid the costs associated with either maintaining the unit or firing the employees. And the employees were able to become self-employed on the condition that their newly formed company would provide transportation for the mother company at no higher a rate than other carriers in the market.[23]

It is interesting that Ackoff describes the same dilemma that Drucker identified in his work, *The New Society*. Ackoff posits that it is a principal obligation of firms to create or maintain employment. But companies must also increase their productivity in order to survive. "But to increase productivity one must usually decrease the labor required per unit of output. Therefore, the requirements for greater productivity and for stable or increasing employment appear to be in conflict."[24] If an enterprise is able to grow it can meet both of these requirements. But this implies that growth is not an end in itself but a means of achieving the real goal of the firm, i.e., to develop. So, Ackoff makes an important distinction between growth and development. And this distinction follows upon the social systems view of the firm. "Growth is an increase in size or number. *Development is an ability and desire to satisfy one's own needs and legitimate desires and those of others. A legitimate desire is one the satisfaction of which does not inhibit the development of someone else.*"[25] This ability to attain the needs and desires of oneself and others is competence. And the ideal limit to the attainment of competence is omnicompetence. A person that is omnicompetent is able to always fulfill all of the needs and desires of themselves and others. Of course, this is never actually attained but represents a limit toward which we must continually strive.[26] If we include the non-economic desire of persons to have status or be treated the way Kant said they should be treated, there is a clear connection between the social systems approach to the firm and the notion of a moral community we found in Kant's ethical theory. Ackoff holds that corporations, not just individuals, have an obligation to promote the development of society and its own stakeholders. This position has a striking similarity to Kant's view that we have a moral obligation to pursue our own perfection and the happiness of others. However, Ackoff sees this obligation as following from the social systems approach to the firm.

The relationship Ackoff draws between the creation and distribution of wealth and the development of persons within and without firms is interesting given Heilbroner's point that within a society of abundance we have the opportunity to transcend economic necessity and pursue economic activity for the sake of other social goals. Ackoff makes the point that wealth contributes to our **stan-**

dard of living but not necessarily to our **quality of life**. Without development, resources do not add to our quality of life. In fact, some people today have identified a sort of "illness" or dis-ease associated with over consumption, what is sometimes called "Affluenza".[27] However, resources can allow persons to develop more rapidly. Development involves learning to make better use of the resources available to us. Ackoff points out that while it is always better to have good tools and materials to build a house; a person whose skills are highly developed can build a better house with poor materials than a poorly skilled person can with very good materials.[28] This is a way of understanding what productivity is. The developed person can make better use of the resources they have and obtain other resources they may need. The result of this analysis is that the creation and distribution of wealth is a means to the broader goal of development. This is the sense of the "Post-Capitalist" society to which Drucker pointed. Capital still exists but is not the most important thing in the economy. The knowledge and skills of the workers making up the economy is. Thus, a democratic social structure contributes to the goal of firms to develop since a democratic structure is the most fruitful in developing its members.

Ackoff goes on to assert that only a democratic political structure is compatible with the social systems approach to the firm. This follows because a social system is a system in which the parts affect the operation of the whole and the whole affects the operation of the parts. This was not the case in the fascist economies studied by Drucker. At best, fascist organizations could be depicted as defective social systems. The danger of the fascist approach was that it provided a semblance of community to its workers by giving them a sense of belonging and purpose. But it did so at the expense of freedom. The flexibility and innovation required by contemporary firms in a knowledge economy depends upon the freedom of their members. Innovation in the economic realm flourishes when the organizations in which people work operate according to the art of the possible, i.e., within democratic organizations.[29]

What is of special interest here is that Ackoff has arrived at a view of the firm or enterprise from a social systems perspective that fits perfectly with Kant's ethical reflection on the freedom of persons and the kingdom of ends. Ackoff actually describes Kant's categorical imperative as fitting a mechanistic ethic rather than a social systemic one because it is an ethic based on the strict application of rules.[30] (An organismic ethic is one that aims at mere survival and so is based on the consequences of actions). But Bowie's account of Kant's ethic within a business context seems to fit very well with Ackoff's promotion of democracy as an implication of the social systems view of the firm. What Ackoff does not appreciate about Kant's categorical imperative is its connection to freedom as a **self-imposed** law. In fact, taking this aspect of Kant's ethic into account, Ackoff's depiction of social systemic ethics fits very well with Kant's approach because it evaluates decisions according to the way they are made and by whom. Allowing workers to participate in the decision making process itself promotes the improvement of their competence. It contributes to their overall development.[31]

It is also the case that Ackoff recognizes that those who are affected by a decision should be able to participate in it. In very large organizations this would necessarily involve the use of representatives since every member of a large organization cannot practically be involved in every decision. Many corporate boards today have representatives from all of the stakeholders including those outside the firm as well as those within it.[32]

The social and ethical demands to recognize the freedom of the person also contribute to the economic or managerial demands of an enterprise in a knowledge economy for innovation and flexibility. Ackoff observes that an organization that fails to recognize that its members have purposes is to restrict their choices and thus to fail to recognize "all the relevant capabilities of their [the enterprise's] parts." Drucker's notion of status captures perfectly both the social systems aspect of this failure and its ethical aspect. They are bound together as the warp and woof of economic existence.

It remains to see what Ackoff considers to be a "completely democratic" system. There are different kinds of democracy, direct and indirect. In general, direct democracy applies to relatively small organizations while indirect democracy applies to larger ones. Ackoff's notion of a circular organization provides a model for a democratization of the workplace that satisfies Drucker's concern to maintain both status and function.

The Circular Organization

Recall that Peter Drucker tried to develop a notion of the plant community as a response to the social needs of workers for a sense of community. It was supposed to recognize the status of workers in a free society. He was eventually forced to abandon that notion in the for-profit sector of the economy because he saw a conflict between the social needs of workers and a functional requirement of business organizations to maintain the authority of management in the decision making process. So, he turned to the non-profit sector of the economy as a source of community within the economic realm. Russell Ackoff can be seen as providing a solution to the structural-functional obstacle Drucker confronted. In developing the social systemic view of the firm and the implications of that view for the democratization of the firm, Ackoff arrived at what he calls "The Circular Organization". This is a model of the firm that provides for both the functional requirement of business organizations identified by Drucker to maintain a rational line of authority and the social requirement of workers to be recognized as having status. It must be remembered that this is not the only kind of structure that might satisfy these demands and it is also important to realize that the particular way that the model is applied in different settings can differ. But it is one that shows very well that it is possible for capitalism and community to coexist in a fruitful way.

Ackoff's concept of the circular organization recognizes that as workers become more highly educated and economically secure their need for participation in the organization of their work-life increases. As Robert Heilbroner pointed out forty-five years ago, "The price of an economy of abundance is the replacement of the traditional economic control mechanism with new kinds of social controls. The central problem of the new society will be to find the means of assuring its own discipline in place of the disappearing force of economic pressure."[33]

The circular organization is a structure that provides for a democratization of the workplace without requiring a radical reorganization, which in itself can be highly disruptive. It recognizes that a hierarchical structure may be necessary to very large firms but provides for the self-direction of all of its members, at least indirectly. It also fosters interaction among its members. According to the social systems approach, it is the interactions among the members of an organization that are significant rather than their individual actions.

According to Ackoff, a democracy has three characteristics. First, there is no ultimate authority. This is what he calls the circularity of power. Secondly, each member must be able to participate (either directly or indirectly) in decisions that affect her or him. And thirdly, the members have the ability to make decisions that affect no one other than the decision makers. "In a democracy, anyone who has authority over others is subject to the collective authority of these others; hence its circularity."[34] The way that the circular organization model accomplishes this is by providing a board for every person in a position of authority. This by itself provides an incentive for flattening organizations. But it can be grafted onto organizations as they currently exist without great disruption. The circularity of the organization is achieved by constituting each board with the manager of the level for which the board exists, the manager's immediate subordinates and her/his immediate supervisor. The top board also includes representatives from the lowest level, thus closing the circle.[35]

One implication of this structure is that if a manager has more than two subordinates, the subordinates have a majority on that board (or a plurality if there are other members added from other interest groups). A board can also add any other members from inside or outside the organization. This allows for all of the stakeholders to be represented. But the number of any single group on the board should not exceed the number of subordinates on the board. And the subordinates should be able to participate in the constitution of the membership of the board. This indicates that the subordinates are the most important group on the board, although they need not make up a majority. At the lowest level of the organization, Ackoff suggests that all of the subordinates be able to be included on the board for their level. If the group at the lowest level is too large to make up a board then that group should be divided into semi-autonomous work groups, each of which has a board. Ackoff notes that this is a model that has been adopted by nearly a dozen government agencies as well as a number of corporations. It is a real-world model that works both economically and socially. It provides for both capitalism and community.

Participation on the boards is to be compulsory for all managers and voluntary for their subordinates. This can actually provide an indicator of how effective a leader a manger is. But perhaps the most important aspect of the circular organization is that it increases the interactions among the different levels of the organization. This is critical in a knowledge economy.

The first reaction people often have to this type of structure is "that's going to require a lot of meetings." But as Ackoff observes, the existence of boards at each level of the organization can actually decrease the need for special groups to facilitate communication.[36] Otherwise, the boards usually meet once a month. There can be extra meetings scheduled for special purposes but the time spent in such meetings is not just wasted time if it contributes to the interaction of the members of the organization. Board meetings may also be canceled if there is nothing on the agenda. If the members of a board are in widely scattered parts of the world they may meet quarterly. (Of course, now there exists the possibility of holding long-distance meetings telephonically or via the internet). If they are in the same office, they can be called any time. In fact, Ackoff notes that one business has a gong that any member of the board can strike to call a meeting.

There are six responsibilities of fully empowered boards. (There can be other advisory boards in addition). These responsibilities include:

1. planning for the unit whose board it is;
2. policymaking for the unit whose board it is;
3. coordinating plans and policies of the immediately lower level;
4. integrating plans and policies—its own and those of its immediately lower level—with those made at higher levels;
5. improving the quality of work life of the subordinates on the board;
6. enhancing and evaluating the performance of the manager whose board it is.[37]

The benefit of planning within a social systemic organization lies in the coordination of the interactions of the members of the group. They must come to see the influence of their actions on the performance of the whole organization. The kind of insular specialization of the traditional production line is actually counterproductive in today's knowledge economy. With respect to policies, a board can establish any policy for its own level as long as it does not affect another level. If a policy does affect another group then approval for the policy must be obtained from that group. This can cause some degree of anxiety for traditional managers who think they must coordinate all of the actions of the organization. In fact, Ackoff describes the reaction of one manager whose workers had eliminated the use of time cards. This also eliminated the need for the manager to direct the workers in terms of their time commitments. It seems obvious that his anxiety may have been grounded in the belief that his own position was relatively superfluous. But it is important to remember that it is the interaction of the members that is of uppermost importance within a social systemic organization, not directing the actions of the workers. Ackoff reports this manager finally relaxed considerably when he realized that if he relied on the expertise of his workers, the productivity of the plant was significantly increased as a result.[38]

We can say that when the status of workers is recognized the quality of work experience rises and typically so does productivity. To keep these people on a clock was undoubtedly experienced by the workers as being held captive to the organization. It is reminiscent of our time in school when as children we watched the clock waiting for a period to be over rather than listening to the teacher. There were probably people spending time trying to figure out how to beat the clock rather than trying to figure out ways to improve their productivity. But the organization also learned in this case how the different parts of the organization interacted. And their awareness of the interactions of the parts of the organization was raised by reconsideration of the policies of the organization. Finally, the connection of the differing boards provides for the effective functioning of the organization.

The responsibility of a board to improve the quality of work life of its members is not a difficult function for the board given that the subordinates of that level typically make up the greatest number of the board's members. So the members are able to make improvements directly rather than their being imposed by an external

authority. Ackoff notes that the management does not always realize how the quality of work experience can best be brought about,
as in the case of workers who decided to "mexicanize" the menu of
their food service.[39]

The way in which a board enhances and evaluates the performance of the manager of a given board may shock many people who
are familiar with the traditional mechanistic or organismic view of
the organization. In good democratic fashion, a manager cannot be
appointed or retain their position without the approval of the members of the board. Doesn't this give the subordinates an inordinate
power over their manager? First, Ackoff notes that the board cannot fire a manager. They can only remove them from their position as manager of that level. We have to consider if this is not
better than a manager continuing to manage people without their
support. That can result in a variety of dysfunctional behaviors
that can undermine productivity, like sabotage or work slowdowns,
etc. If workers have buy-in because they participated in the
placement of a manager, they have an incentive to make that manager look good.[40]

In addition, the subordinates of a board can meet periodically to
determine what positive changes a manager can make to improve
the workers' performance. The group then meets with a facilitator
to present the suggestions of the group. In a way, this approach is
the inverse of the "Stupid Hour". I suppose it could be called the
"Let's Try to be Smart Hour". One such group suggested that their
superior should take advantage of his vacation time so that the
other members of the group would not feel guilty in taking advantage of theirs.[41]

The example of the vacation allowance is a good one for illustrating how important **interaction** is within an organization. The
existence of multiple boards formalizes this aspect of the organization and turns it into a benefit. If a manger rejects a proposal from
the subordinates, the manager must provide an explanation for the
rejection. This often involves a constraint from a higher level of
which the workers were not previously aware. Since workers have
representation at the higher levels they can pursue the issue at the
higher levels if they wish. But even if they are not able to get what
they want, the understanding of the constraints involved usually
helps them to accept the situation that exists.

What is clear from this activity of the boards is that the function of managers is radically altered within a social systemically conceived organization. Ackoff notes that these improvement sessions, as he calls them, can make for a greater collaboration between management and workers. The traditional relationship is altered so that the knowledge and skills of the workers is brought to the fore. It is for this reason that Ackoff holds that managers are not to supervise their subordinates, but rather, they are supposed to promote an environment in which workers can maximize the exercise of their skills and capacities.[42]

What Ackoff is looking for in the creation of a circular organization is a change in the culture of the organization. An important part of the implementation of this design is the creation of an internal market within the organization. But this goes beyond our area of interest. It is interesting that Ackoff sees the movement to a circular organization is tantamount to moving from an autocratic to a democratic political model.[43] That is essentially the same problematic that Peter Drucker saw during the Second World War. The difference is that now that struggle is one that has to take place within business organizations.

What we can see is that the most advanced of managerial theories comports perfectly with the moral theory set out by Norman Bowie. The information age has brought about a confluence of economic and moral requirements. A democratic organization or plant community that recognizes the status of workers also promotes a high degree of work satisfaction and thus contributes to the productivity of workers.

NOTES

1. Russell L. Ackoff, *The Democratic Corporation*, Oxford University Press, 1994, pp. 7-8.
2. Ibid., p. 12.
3. Ibid.
4. Ibid.
5. Ibid.
6. Ibid., p. 13.
7. Ibid., pp. 13-14.
8. Ibid., p. 37.
9. Ibid., p. 16.
10. Ibid., pp. 18-21.
11. Ibid., p. 22.
12. Ibid., p. 23.
13. Ibid., p. 26.
14. Ibid., p. 78, emphasis in the original.
15. Ibid., p. 27.
16. Ibid., p. 28.
17. Ibid., p. 29.
18. Ibid., p. 30.
19. Ibid., p. 31.
20. *The New Face of Work in America: Jobs Not What They Used to Be.* Films for the Humanities, 1996.
21. Russell L. Ackoff, *The Democratic Corporation*, Oxford University Press, 1994, p. 77.
22. Ibid., p. 31.
23. Ibid., p. 43.
24. Ibid., p. 44.
25. Ibid., p. 45, emphasis in the original.
26. Ibid., p. 48.
27. See Juliet Schor, *The Overspent American*, Perennial, 1999. Also, John De Graaf, David Wann, Thomas H. Naylor, David Horsey, Scott Simon, *Affluenza*, Berrett-Koehler, Publishers, 2002.
28. Russell L. Ackoff, *The Democratic Corporation*, Oxford University Press, 1994, p. 47.
29. See Russell L. Ackoff, *The Democratic Corporation*, Oxford University Press, p. 32.
30. Russell L. Ackoff, *The Democratic Corporation*, Oxford University Press, p. 53.
31. Ibid., p. 56.
32. Ibid., p. 57.
33. Robert L. Heilbroner, *The Future as History*, Grove Press Inc., 1961, p. 153.

34. Russell L. Ackoff, *The Democratic Corporation*, Oxford University Press, p. 117.

35. See Ackoff's illustration on p. 119 of *The Democratic Corporation*.

36. Russell L. Ackoff, *The Democratic Corporation*, Oxford University Press, p. 126.

37. Ibid., p. 124.

38. Ibid., pp. 126-127.

39. Ibid., p. 129.

40. Ibid.

41. Ibid., p. 131

42. Ibid., emphasis in the original.

43. Ibid., p. 140.

Chapter V
Aesthetics and High Performance Organizations

One of the innovations that Russell Ackoff has introduced into management theory is a focus on aesthetic matters. He argues that as the economy develops, the level of wealth rises, and people obtain greater educational attainments, they become dissatisfied with monotonous and meaningless work. Within the environment of a knowledge economy work must not only provide a living wage but satisfaction, and even fun. This is necessary as a stimulus to the innovation that is essential to a knowledge economy. Ackoff provides an instructive example because it applies to the owners of a business. He points to a business that was run by three owners. Since the business was well established, it did not require much effort on their part to run it. In order to introduce some challenge to the task of operating their business, they eventually added a new product that required concentrated effort on their part. In the end, this innovative process stimulated everyone in the business, improving their productivity and the quality of their work experience.[1]

This is an example that illustrates very well the point that Ackoff makes concerning the need for social systems to develop and not simply grow. The people involved in this process were able to increase their competence, which then had the effect of increasing their productivity. Trying to simply increase profits by cutting costs, and perhaps sacrificing quality in the process, is a shortcut that may have short-term benefits, but in the long run is usually counterproductive. In this vein, Ackoff provides another example of a firm that was faced with a competitor that gained market share by price-cutting. Rather than cutting its production costs, this company retained its commitment to high quality and eventually regained its market share, and even gained more.[2]

When businesses were conceived as being machines or organisms it was not necessary to make work fulfilling or satisfying. In the social systems environment it is necessary to do so. Ackoff believes it has become necessary to integrate work with play and learning. This involves jettisoning the old Protestant work ethic that saw work as necessarily unpleasant and perhaps unsatisfying. The ascetic ideal of that ethic must now be replaced with a new ideal of work as being a potential source of self-fulfillment. As Heilbroner pointed out, in a society of abundance, the motivations of workers and the sources of social discipline will be different from those of the early industrial revolution. According to Ackoff, "Today we increasingly believe that everyone is entitled to work that not only satisfies but that contributes to the development of the worker."[3] For many people who have attended college in the United States this may hearken back to a minor classic that is often required reading in business ethics, *Small Is Beautiful*. In that work, E.F. Schumacher described what he called "Buddhist Economics". According to Buddhist economics, work has a three-fold function. First, it is supposed to help the worker to overcome her ego centeredness by working cooperatively with others. It thus has a beneficial effect on a person's character. Secondly, it is supposed to develop the skills of the worker. And thirdly, it is supposed to produce goods and services for a becoming human existence.[4] This was a remarkably prescient view of work. For it applies especially well to the present-day information economy. And it is fascinating that Schumacher chose to depict the value of work in terms of a Buddhist ethic. Perhaps it was his way of trying to overcome the old Protestant ethic regarding work.

Of course, Ackoff holds that there is a close tie between the quality of work life and the quality of products people produce. That seems intuitively self-evident. So, he wants to link quality of work life to the attempt to improve product quality. According to Ackoff, the aesthetic aspect of decision making is integral to the improvement of the quality of work life. Now, for Ackoff, the aesthetic aspect of decision making is really the style of the decision maker. This includes the preferences of the decision maker, which is distinct from the efficiency of the person's activities. In other words, the style of the decision maker has to do with the satisfaction the person derives from what they do. There is, in addition, a second non-utilitarian aspect of decision making, i.e., the sense of progress a person feels in approaching their developmental ideal. We must recall that Ackoff takes the ideal endpoint of personal development to be a state of omni-competence. But omni-competence can only be approached as people exercise their powers and grow in their ability to achieve their goals. So, Ackoff holds that the quality of work life increases most to the degree that people are able to design their own work.[5]

Within the social systems view of the workplace, the value of self-determination that Kant found to be the basis of the dignity of persons and the moral requirement to treat all persons with respect turns out to also be the basis for the development of workers and the organizations for which they work. It is all of a piece. For, according to the social systems view of the firm, business organizations are made up parts (persons) that have purposes of their own. They cannot check their humanity or their personhood at the door when they go to work for a company. And companies ought not to treat them as though they should. In fact, companies are better off if they recognize the humanity of their workers. Peter Drucker recognized a long time ago that if workers are treated as members of a community, as having status, then the social functioning of organizations can be enhanced. To his credit, Ackoff recognized this. His argument that we ought not to impose quality of life improvements on workers but find ways to allow them to make their own improvements recognizes that a confluence of aesthetics and ethics is good management policy.[6]

Ackoff promotes what he calls "Interactive Idealized Design". This approach recognizes that persons will inevitably insert their own values in the designs they create. This includes both aesthetic and ethical values. And that is not a bad thing. Ackoff distinguishes between bounded and unbounded idealized design. Bounded idealized design proceeds on the assumption that the unit to be redesigned was completely destroyed last night. The question then is, "if you could design this unit in any way you wished, how would you do it?" Now, another assumption is that the environment within which the unit exists has not changed. The result is supposed to be an ideal design for those designing the unit.

There are three constraints on the design process. First, it must be technically feasible. Second, the design must be operationally feasible. That is, it must be able to function effectively within the environment within which it exists. And third, the system to be designed must have the ability to adapt to changes in the environment. This effectively builds learning into the system. Unbounded idealized design allows the designers to change the containing system of the unit to be redesigned, as long as it only affects the way the redesigned unit operates. This approach allows for a maximum of participation in the design process.[7]

In implementing the design, the task is to reach as close an approximation of the ideal as possible. Ackoff asserts that this kind of quality of work life approach can save plants that are being closed and bring back to life organizations that are dead. This is because those involved in the redesign of their work, find the very process to be exhilarating. In the end, their work can become more meaningful and enriching. And, of course, the redesign of work can introduce significant cost savings. Here Ackoff points to a case of an aluminum plant in Tennessee that had the occasion to honor two of its employees who introduced a cost-saving measure based on their many years of experience in the plant. When Ackoff asked them how long they knew of this potential improvement, they both lowered their heads and replied that they knew of it for some fifteen years. By their own account, the reason they had never spoken up before is that the SOB's in the plant hierarchy had never asked them.[8]

We can readily understand their attitude. They had not been treated as members of the community, as having status. As a result, their dignity had been bruised. But now we know that the knowledge of the workers is the most valuable asset a firm has. Tapping that knowledge requires that we allow them to exercise their freedom to apply their knowledge. Leonard Swap illustrates this by pointing to a study of eight U.S. biotechnology firms that were divided into high and low innovation groups based on an analysis of their cycle times, i.e., the speed of bringing a product to market. The "ability of management to create a sense of community in the workplace was the key differentiating factor. Highly innovative units behaved as focused communities, while less innovative units behaved more like traditional bureaucratic depart-ments."[9]

One company that has been very successful in forming such communities of innovation is IDEO. IDEO is a company that has become well known for its innovative techniques of idea creation. And one of the interesting aspects of this business is its recognition of the aesthetic dimension of work. When Tom Peters discovered IDEO his reaction was a little impolitic.

> Following a half-day tour, I recall clearly bouncing in the front door of our office and saying to our receptionist, the first person I encountered, 'It's finally happened, I've seen a company where I can imagine work-ing!' (In retrospect, I guess that was a frightening thing to say to her).
>
> The company in question was IDEO (actually, at the time, David Kelly Design). And I'd been bowled over by the spirit and sense of playfulness that invaded every aspect of its stellar—wildly creative—work.[10]

If that is the way a visitor responds after a half-day visit we can imagine how those who work at IDEO must feel about working there. Ackoff would concur that the sense of playfulness is a good sign of the creativity of the work environment.

Tom Kelly reports that IDEO has been on the "front lines" of over three thousand new product development programs. They are known for creating the original Apple mouse and the Palm V or-ganizer. But they have also helped many companies reinvent their organizations and have helped in the creation of new start-ups. They also took on the redesign of the shopping cart for *Nightline*, illustrating their methods of innovation on television. After it aired, they were inundated with calls about their approach to idea creation.

> The morning after the *Nightline* segment ran, our phones wouldn't stop ringing. I took dozens of calls from executives around the country who'd seen the show. Most of them didn't give a damn about shopping carts. Instead, they wanted to know more about the process we used to bring the cart into being. One CEO told me that he understood, for the first time, what creativity really meant and how it could be managed in a business environment.[11]

After many years of experience in innovating both products and organizations IDEO has tried to develop a schema for innovation, a difficult thing to do given that spontaneity is at the heart of innovation. But an important part of Kelly's treatment of innovation is that it is not just a set of practices but a culture that permeates an organization. And, it is interesting how Kelly emphasizes the team character of innovation. "Our 'secret formula' is actually not very formulaic. It's a blend of methodologies, work practices, culture, and infrastructure. Methodology alone is not enough."[12] As Ikujiro Nonaka explains, idea creation is a movement from tacit knowledge to explicit knowledge. In a knowledge economy the problem of management is to live with the creative destruction of innovation on a daily basis.

> Managers everywhere recognize the serendipitous quality of innovation. Executives at these Japanese companies are managing that serendipity to the benefit of the company, its employees, and its customers.
> The centerpiece of the Japanese approach is the recognition that creating new knowledge is not simply a matter of "processing" objective information. Rather, it depends upon tapping the tacit and often highly subjective insights, intuitions, and hunches of individual employees and making those insights available for testing and use by the company as a whole. The key to this process is personal commitment, the employees' sense of identity with the enterprise and its mission.[13]

Eileen Appelbaum points out that some innovative management techniques have been introduced into organizations precisely in order to tap this implicit knowledge of workers.

> Managers have used work reform to try to get workers to apply their creativity and imagination to their work and to exploit, in the interests of the organization, their intimate and often unconscious knowledge of the work process. This type of behavior is particularly difficult to elicit and use effectively with traditional hierarchical managerial strategies.[14]

Among the elements of the methodology of innovation as practiced at IDEO are:

> 1) Understand the market, the client, the technology, and the perceived constraints on the problem.

2) Observe real people in real-life situations to find out what makes them tick: what confuses them, what they like, what they hate, where they have latent needs not addressed by current products and services.
3) Visualize new-to-the-world concepts and customers who will use them.
4) Evaluate and refine the prototypes in a series of quick iterations.
5) Implement the new concept for commercialization.[15]

Brainstorming is an essential aspect of the success at innovation at IDEO. Although Kelly thinks it is better to refer to the activity as "brainstormers". From the perspective of this study, the team character of brainstormers is one of its most significant aspects. Sharing ideas creates a synergy that is missing from the model of the lone inventor. And the aesthetic dimension as well as the sheer fun of interacting with a creative group of people determines the success of the present-day information organization.

Sports utility shopping carts. Velcro diapers. A privacy curtain to hide those embarrassing purchases. These are just a few of the wacky ideas hatched during our Nightline shopping cart brainstormer. I can't emphasize enough what these flights of fancy do for the team. They remind everybody that this isn't like work, that anything goes, and that we're going to have a lot of fun while we solve our problems.[16]

Morale is kept high at IDEO by fostering a culture of fun and excitement. Field trips, off-site conferences, and playing hooky to see a movie or visit a museum are part of the work experience at IDEO. The completion of projects is often celebrated with special gifts for team members. And an end-of-year party only brings out the play of imagination that typifies work at IDEO. "We once managed to take temporary possession of Moffet Field's blimp hangar. Amid the airplanes, a zydeco band jammed, while we rollerbladed through an indoor space the size of seven football fields."[17] But the playfulness of the work environment at IDEO is not just a matter of maintaining high morale. It is part of the culture of exploring borders that makes IDEO a high performance enterprise.

IDEO has several different locations in the Palo Alto area and has developed several different studio teams that are housed at the

different locations. One of the significant aspects of team formation at IDEO is that the members of a team are able to choose their
team leader. And the team leader is able to choose their work site.
After a period of time, the teams are changed. In this way, IDEO
is able to form "Hot Groups" of highly creative and motivated
people. Link up the freedom of persons to shape their work experience and add meaningful work and sparks are bound to fly.

> We believe the strongest teams take root when individuals are
> given the chance of picking what groups they work with and even oc-
> casionally what projects they work on. That way, passion fuels the fire.
> For example, we were recently asked to develop a kid's car seat. We
> asked for volunteers, and dozens of employees stepped forward. One
> of the dads who volunteered was so concerned about safety that he'd
> already bought ten different car seats for his three kids...IDEO's car
> seat dad was helping to ensure the safety of his own children, as well as
> that of thousands of others. Not a bad reason to get out of bed in the
> morning.[18]

The organization of the work space at IDEO is as innovative as
its products. In fact, organizing the work space is itself a team
building opportunity. But there is also a great deal of individuality
in each person's office. Indeed, Kelly believes that their offices
work because everyone has a say in their organization. But this
individuality is balanced by a concrete sense of community. To
this end, the offices of a given team are referred to as a neighborhood. The central desk for team meetings is the neighborhood
park. And the identity of the group is fostered by encouraging
teams to develop their own icon.

In an interview, David Kelly notes that since IDEO has seven
different office locations around Palo Alto (and a number of others
around the world), it is important to resist the temptation to follow
the advice of the bean counters; that they have seven different re-
ceptionists and these could be reduced to one if the company con-
solidated its office space in a single location (unemploying six people in the process). That would detract from the sense of community that workers experience because there is not a single set of
rules that are imposed from on high. Rather, each group is able to
have a sense of ownership over their work environment by giving
it their own individual character.[19] Individuality and community

are not antithetical to one another. In fact, they are mutually supporting.

> We believe in the importance of neighborhoods and community in fostering innovation. Try creating spaces that draw workers in and encourage interaction...Everybody who lives by that 'park' can see at a glance whether their neighbors are at home, but they can also slide translucent Lexan barn doors closed if they need to buckle down and work privately on something. It's a wonderful mix of community and privacy that seems to offer much of the seclusion of traditional offices without the separation.[20]

In the San Francisco office a wall was removed and replaced by a transparent structure that allows people to view the bay and bridge. The office manager's space was moved from this location and replaced with what is now called the Lookout, which includes lunch tables, a kitchen area, and a library. This use of the space supports innovation and eliminates the old hierarchical use of space that treats favored spots as rewards for the executives of the company. "Should that great view go to the CEO or the company lunchroom?"[21] If the people who work there have a voice in organizing the space, the answer is clear.

High Performance Organizations

Eileen Appelbaum and Rosemary Batt have made the argument that American businesses have sought to produce high performance organizations by applying a pot pourri of management practices that may or may not produce the desired results. The idea of self-managed teams derives from the socio-technical approach of the British and Norwegians. The Japanese approach to lean production introduced such innovations as quality circles, total quality engineering, and just-in-time production. The Italians and Germans have introduced flexible specialization.[22] One or more of these approaches is typically blended with an American human relations approach. This eclectic approach may have the advantage of allowing for a variety of approaches that may be applied to different environments but may not be effective outside the specialized environments in which they were developed. It is therefore incumbent upon individual firms to experiment with a variety of the best practices available to produce positive results. For example, Appelbaum et al., found that a particular bundle of practices in the steel industry were efficacious. "In the steel industry we identify bundles of practices that form coherent work systems and increased productivity. We show that these systems have a greater effect on productivity than their components do individually."[23]

Out of the range of varying approaches taken by contemporary American businesses, Appelbaum and Batt have identified two main strategies. One prominent strategy adopted by many American businesses is a version of lean production. This approach emphasizes the kinds of criteria recognized by the Baldrige Award. It makes use of a "top-management-driven" quality system. The second approach is more decentralized and is labeled "American Team Production". "It combines the principles of Swedish sociotechnical systems and self-directed work with those of quality engineering."[24] They observe that both approaches have produced improvements in performance. They both involve certain risks as well. The risk associated with a decentralized approach is that there can be uneven execution and synchronization within the firm and the risk associated with centralization is a lack of autonomous effort on the part of the employees, which can depress innovation.[25]

Now, even though these two approaches have produced gains in performance for firms, Appelbaum and Batt observe that the outcomes for workers are different in the two models. "The American version of team production provides employees with greater discretion or autonomy, more employment security, and a greater guarantee of a share in any performance gains."[26] From the perspective of Kantian ethical theory it would seem that the version of American team production is superior. So, if it is true that it produces production gains comparable to that of lean production, there is a good reason to adopt it from an ethical point of view.

But what about the risks of the team approach? The circular organization model seems to provide for the very coordination that is at issue in the team approach. It allows for the diffusion of information and coordination of action that is at risk in the team approach. Appelbaum and Batt provide an example of a firm that developed what appears to be a circular organization model or something closely akin to it. "In 1992, the CWA, IBEW, and

AT&T, in an agreement known as the 'Workplace of the Future,' agreed to create a joint structure...The agreement anticipates joint union-management participation in four representative bodies at three levels of the corporation: the workplace, the business unit, and corporate levels."[27] This structure was supposed to provide for "interactive planning, both top down and bottom up".[28] Unfortunately, the structure was apparently used to soften the blow of a massive downsizing.[29] So it may be an example of a lack of good will. But Appelbaum & Batt note that this type of structure can be seen as a peculiarly American form of management/union partnership. "At Xerox, Saturn, and Corning, a distinctively American form of 'partnership' between plant management and the union has emerged, which emphasizes the development of a 'shared business vision' and joint union-management committees **at every level of the organization**."[30]

A well formed structure can foster good will within an organization. BellSouth successfully combined a quality program with an employee-involvement program that had the effect of improving the relation between management and labor.

> The QWL program has been popular among employees in the Bell system because it represents the first time that managers agreed to participate with employees in problem solving around workplace issues. Although committees initially ended up dealing with issues that concerned the quality of employees' work life more than the quality of their work performance, the committees have contributed to improved labor-management relations and employee goodwill at the local level.[31]

Appelbaum and Batt observe that while the lean production model seems to apply particularly in non-union settings, the team approach seems to work best in unionized firms. They have noted that unions make a contribution on the human relations side of a decentralized organization.

> Where unions have the organizational capacity and leadership to become involved in production decisions, they appear to provide an organizational asset not available in nonunion settings. In decentralized systems, joint union-management structures can improve the coordination and diffusion of the high-performance work systems, ensure consistency across work units, and persuade or pressure resistant employ-

ees or managers to participate in ways that top management is unable to do through internal channels in the firm.[32]

Indeed, Appelbaum et al., point out that in the 1980's unions often initiated the kinds of changes that make up a high performance work system.[33] High-performance work systems (HPWSs) are made up of a cluster of workplace innovations that include worker incentives, skills, and the opportunity to participate in decision making that improve an organization's performance.[34] HPWSs recognize that the social organization of work must be coordinated with the technological framework of the work environment. In the automobile industry, it is not the most technologically advanced plants that are necessarily the most productive. Rather, it is the plants that are able to integrate technological means and social organization that achieve the highest productivity and product quality.[35]

Since workers require more developed skills to do their jobs in a decentralized work environment they need incentives to invest in the development of their skills, especially since there is great difficulty in directly measuring this component of their contribution to work, and some of their skills may be firm specific. It is for this reason that Appelbaum et al., suggest that employment security, as well as gain sharing, are essential in a HPWS.[36] (As I write this in the summer of 2004, the U.S. economy is showing softness on a couple of fronts. While corporations are seeing healthy profits, workers' wages have not risen to keep up with inflation. According to Jeremy Rifkin, "Even during the rapid economic recovery of the second half of 2003, the average hourly wage of nonsupervisory jobs in American offices and factories went up only 3 cents, according to the Bureau of Labor Statistics—barely enough to keep even with inflation. This is the slowest wage growth America has experienced in forty years."[37] In addition, gasoline prices are high. And so, consumer spending is off. It seems that if corporate profits were more broadly shared with workers they would have greater purchasing power, which is essential to the strength of the economy). From a moral perspective, a firm ought to compensate its employees at a higher rate if it enjoys higher profits.[38] Appelbaum et al., find that HPWSs tend to have significantly higher wages.[39] As a result, we can see that HPWSs conform to the economic requirements of a knowledge economy inasmuch as they increase productivity and can lower some costs.[40] They also conform to the ethical requirements of Kant's ethical theory to provide more meaningful work and job security. Appelbaum et al., note that even if the development of a HPWS does not raise wages, it may save jobs.[41]

> Using a socio-technical approach, employee-management task groups redesigned jobs so as to convert an assembly-line system for processing copyright applications into a 'product-line' approach in which semi-autonomous teams handled all of the paperwork for the product line in question. Turnaround time dropped from as much as four months to two weeks. After four years, the labor-management committee reported a 15 percent gain in productivity, which saved taxpayers $5 million...[42]

Appelbaum et al., draw upon examples of high performance works systems from the U.S. steel industry that are instructive. They note that market forces led steel mills in the United States to develop high performance work systems, which involves welding human resource practices and technology into a coherent whole. At the same time, it is important to realize that the mix of practices can vary from one mill to another, depending on the particular culture of the organization. Among the market forces at work was a demand for higher quality and on-time delivery. So the changes in work organization were largely driven by customer demand. Steel companies in the United States have been led to give greater weight to lowering defect rates, conforming to the specifications of their customers, and providing consistent on-time delivery. These demands could not be met by carrying out the traditional cost saving measures. It was necessary to innovate the work place to create a high performance environment. Work teams and problem-solving teams became necessary to involve the front line workers in achieving the goals of the organization. Of course, these kinds of teams can also provide significant cost savings as well as improve quality.[43] In addition, "Mills have also begun to adopt human resource practices that build mutual commitment between workers and managers and that support the changes in work organization, including employment security agreements and quality incentives."[44]

These are exactly the kinds of innovations that we described in the Kantian workplace. It is especially interesting that it took the necessity of market forces to introduce a greater level of freedom into these workplaces. According to Appelbaum et al., the steelworkers union, the USWA, has negotiated cooperative partnership agreements with some steel producers that include what Bowie called open book management.[45] The unions have also been able to gain representation on the boards of a number of companies. The unions have an interest in reforming the work environment in the direction of a HPWS in order to preserve jobs.[46] One example Appelbaum et al., describe is a union that participated in the reorganization of jobs in the electro-galvanizing area of a large sheet mill. A team of union representatives, managers, and workers were able to improve the operation of the unit by creating a new position that required retraining of the workers. A job security agreement and production bonuses helped to give the workers an incentive to participate in the retraining and the unit has become more productive as a result.[47]

What is especially noteworthy here is that some of the requirements of a Kantian workplace, like job security, can be helpful in overcoming the resistance to change experienced by some workers, as in this example. The changes that are associated with a democratization of the workplace can give rise to a great deal of anxiety. Russell Ackoff noted that reforming an organization can be disruptive. But if people are treated the way Kant's ethical theory says they ought to be treated, the transition can often be smoothed out.

It is interesting that according to Appelbaum et al., work teams in the steel industry are not very different from traditional work crews. What is different is the **interaction** of the workers among themselves and with their supervisors. This is precisely the point that Ackoff made about organizations conceived as systems. "What distinguishes a team of operators from a traditional work crew is the frequent interaction and collaboration among team members and the relationship of workers to their supervisors."[48] In contrast to the formal structure of the circular organization, at some mills there is not a formal team structure but work groups end up working as self-directed teams because of the scheduling of work at the mill.[49] What is interesting about this circumstance is that there is not the formal structure that Ackoff's circular organization provides and yet there is effectively a democratization of the workplace having many of the elements we have seen associated with such an organization.[50]

Steel mills have necessarily become learning organizations because the jobs at contemporary mills have become more demanding of the knowledge of workers. And so, today's mills provide more formal training than previously. In the past, workers have gained their knowledge by on-the-job training. Now, many companies provide cross-training for their new employees so they can develop a variety of skills. They also often provide training in team-building, all of which represents a considerable investment in the workers.[51] With this kind of extensive investment in its workers it is clear why some organizations today are willing to provide for job security. It also seems clear that it would be unjust to not pass along some of the gains from improved performance to the workers who have invested so much of themselves in their job.

Appelbaum et al., note that some mills have instituted pay schemes that tie workers' income to performance. One of them is reminiscent of the scheme we described in chapter three that was advocated by Lester C. Thurow in *The Zero-Sum Solution*.

> One nonunion steel mill we visited recently changed ownership. The first action taken by the new owner was to implement a pay-for-performance plan. Wages were reduced by 15 percent, and an incentive system based on production in the melt shop and the rolling mill was added to compensation. Management reports that annual take-home pay increased 10 percent over the previous year.[52]

Now, there are problems with this approach. As Appelbaum et al., observe, this approach places the risk on the shoulders of the workers. As such, it would seem that there should be a commensurate increase in their compensation level. It is also possible to even out the payments to a certain extent by making the performance payments on a quarterly basis or perhaps bi-annually. In this way the workers would not see a weekly or monthly variation in their pay package. Finally, it seems that in this case the workers were not involved in the design of the remuneration system. Imposing such a system (heteronomy of the will) is likely to produce resistance. If they had been allowed to participate in the design of the system (autonomy of the will) they would probably have bought into it more readily than they did.

Appelbaum et al., provide another example of a nonunion mill at which one third of the worker's compensation is a fixed wage and two thirds is given out in the form of incentive pay. These workers are some of the highest paid workers in the industry. This kind of incentive pay often works very well with a democratization of the workplace.[53]

Other examples can be found in the apparel industry. Appelbaum et al., argue that market changes have led some apparel manufacturers to reform their work organization so as to be able to achieve fast turnaround times and avoid the slowdowns associated with the traditional production system. Developing a high performance work system can compensate for the lower wage rates that are found overseas. "Some industry analysts argue that the lower inventory levels, lower risks, and faster inventory turnaround made possible by this quick response could save enough to compensate for a 25 to 35 percent differential in wholesale prices between domestic-and-foreign produced apparel."[54] These manufacturers have found that automation and lower labor costs do not represent an adequate response to the competitive pressures introduced by globalization. What was needed in addition was to innovate the workplace. And what is especially interesting is that some apparel manufacturers were committed to keeping their operations in the United States, despite the pressure to ship their operations overseas. They were able to turn the new market situation to their advantage by innovating the work place.[55]

In response to the demand for short lead times in the production of clothing, retailers developed a system called "Lean Retailing". This involved applying a point-of-sale inventory control system so that an order could be made when inventories reached a certain level. This actually gave an advantage to domestic producers. Perhaps those that have moved their production processes overseas for the sake of cheap labor have simply taken the easy way out, so to speak, rather than doing the hard work of thinking through their production process.[56]

The possibility of short lead times provided for an expansion of styles and selling seasons. The goal became to build flexibility and responsiveness into the production process. "Modular production" is a form of high performance work system in the apparel industry that includes increased training, new incentives, and team work.[57]

We have already seen that there is a demand for meaningful work in a Kantian workplace. This procedure allows for a more meaningful work experience than the traditional approach because the workers are able to complete the production of an identifiable whole product. (Compare this to the work of the spot-welder in chapter three). Here there is task variety, which has reduced the costs associated with carpal tunnel injuries.[58] And the need for quality inspectors is greatly reduced because the workers carry out continuous inspection of their own work. That is, they monitor themselves. To a certain extent, they are self-directing.[59] It is almost as if the workers have the role of owners in a traditional workplace, having the responsibilities that come with ownership. Undoubtedly, the workers in this environment have a greater sense of ownership over their jobs and thus have a greater sense of status within the organization. Kant would likely consider this mode of work organization more in line with the demands of the moral law to treat persons with respect than the traditional mode of organization.

Needless to say, the demands on workers are greater inasmuch as they must develop a wider range of skills, which may include basic repairs on sewing machines. But the value of a HPWS lies in the skills of the workers who may innovate their own workplace.

> Employers need more skilled and flexible employees who can work in a more varied and rapidly changing environment and who can contribute ideas and suggestions for improving manufacturing processes...Personal conflicts within modules can be a serious problem; therefore, this form of high-performance organization puts a premium on social skills.[60]

As Schumacher said about the Buddhist conception of work, one of the positive features of work is that it can help us to overcome our ego-centeredness by working cooperatively with others. Social skills are a key to the functioning of a HPWS. That is one reason why conceiving of an organization as a community is helpful in the workplace of the new information economy. Of course, conflict is possible within a community. But conflict can be useful in a HPWS. Some people see creative abrasion as a critical component of innovation within a team context.[61] While conflict by itself is not positive, conflict and a process of conflict resolution can be beneficial.[62]

Many plants that employ the module approach have developed a system of remuneration based on the productivity of teams. This gives the team members an incentive to improve not only their own productivity but also to contribute to the overall productivity of the team. It can enhance teamwork and can even supplant the need for the traditional manager to monitor individuals. Peer pressure takes the place of the traditional manager. By tying the wage to productivity, the workers get periodic feedback on their productivity. They also have a sense that they participate in the gains that they make.[63] Appelbaum et al., point to a U.S. company that moved some of its production to the Caribbean only to find that they were not able to meet their stringent delivery requirements. After changing the domestic production process to modules they found that the domestic production was more efficient in meeting time and quality quotas.[64] Another company that introduced modules found that "the module system was much more efficient for shorter production runs and allowed much more precise delivery planning for both small and short orders. Throughput time on a typical product had fallen from three days to forty minutes, and, although labor costs had not changed, base wages increased by about a fifth."[65] Still another company was able to reduce the time required to produce one item from ten days to one hour and cut labor costs by eliminating quality inspectors and other supervisory personnel.[66] Finally,

> Another manager introduced modules in a plant that produces one item. The introduction of modules reduced the throughput time from two and a half days to 150 minutes. Although the cost per unit went up by almost 3 percent, the manager was able to raise the base wage by 20 percent. This increase improved the plant's ability to recruit workers.[67]

Obviously, it is more difficult to recruit good workers if the work is very tedious and repetitive. In a knowledge economy the challenge is to provide a working environment that attracts good workers who will possibly continue to innovate the workplace. Appelbaum et al., report that in the apparel industry the opportunity to participate raised the level of trust among workers but working in self-directed teams did not positively affect their work satisfaction. So, the results of a HPWS can be mixed and can vary in different industries.

In the Medical Electronic Instruments industry the problem has been to link manufacturing with the design process and marketing. The introduction of HPWSs in this industry has had the effect of increasing the communication between these different segments within organizations. ECGSystems, for example, employs teams for production and for problem-solving within the company. They have developed cross-functional teams, like IDEO, that participate in both design and the manufacturing of their products.[68]

Once again, we see the confluence of several positive factors in a HPWS. In the case of steel, workers are able to work as members of a community because they have a commitment from the company to not resort to massive layoffs as a short-term cost cutting measure. They are not a mere means for the company to dispose of as they wish. In the steel, apparel, and medical technology industries, workers have meaningful participation in the decision making process and also share in the gains from the improvements in their performance. And, not surprisingly, the participation of workers on teams is correlated with higher wages.[69]

The economic requirements of the organization and the social requirements of the workers are compatible with each other. Capitalism and community works. And to top it all off, this way of organizing the work environment seems to conform to the moral requirements of Kant's ethical theory. To the extent that workers are able to participate in the decision making process and share in the gains (as well as the burdens) of their shared work experience, to that extent we approach Kant's ideal of a kingdom of ends within the workplace, where the status of workers is recognized in a concrete way.

To sum up, there is the **possibility** of a "virtuous dynamic", as Appelbaum et al., put it, in the knowledge economy whereby the practices that are adopted for the sake of improving economic performance also have the effect of improving the work experience and benefits of its employees.[70] And part of the reason for this fortuitous confluence lies in the information technology that has come to define the knowledge economy. For, a technology not only al-

ters the physical environment of a society but brings with it a requirement for a certain culture. Jeremy Rifkin has described the
shift in the culture of work that the introduction of the clock
brought about at the dawn of the industrial age as a mechanism to
coordinate the use of new productive technologies.

> Work bells, and later the work clock, became the instrument of the
> merchants and factory owners to control the work time of their labor-
> ers. Historian Jacques Le Goff remarks that here was the introduction
> of a radical new tool to assert power and control over the masses. He
> writes, 'The communal clock was an instrument of economic, social,
> and political domination wielded by the merchants who ran the com-
> mune.'
> Whereas in the craft trades and in farming, the workers had set the
> pace of activity, in the new factory system, the machinery dictated the
> tempo. That tempo was incessant, unrelenting, and exacting. The in-
> dustrial production mode was, above all else, methodical. Its rhythm
> mirrored the rhythm of the clock. The new worker was expected to
> surrender his time completely to the new factory rhythm. He was to
> show up on time, work at the pace the machine set, and then leave at
> the appointed time. Subjective time considerations had no place inside
> the factory. There, objective time—machine time—ruled supreme.[71]

There are some who hold that the cultural requirements of
modern technology are, on the whole, harmful.[72] But there exists
at least the possibility that as we "informate" our society, as Shoshana Zuboff would say, we will at the same time be led to provide
for a more humanly satisfying work environment.

> Several studies provide evidence that information technology used to
> 'informate' (Zuboff 1988) jobs is complementary with high-
> performance work organization and human resource management
> (HRM) practices...Because of the complementarities or synergies be-
> tween workplace practices and information technology, the falling price
> of information technology increases not only firms' use of such tech-
> nology, but the probability that they will implement other high-
> performance practices.[73]

If we were to take advantage of this social possibility, as Heilbroner put it, we could do what Peter Drucker suggested, i.e., develop a non-economic society that is based on the human need for
community. In the process, we could approach the just society that
is the goal of Kant's ethical theory. "Overall, our results suggest

that in manufacturing, the introduction of HPWSs lead to win-win outcomes for plants and workers."[74] This is why I have said we can have our economic cake and eat it too. For, in the knowledge economy, it is possible to align the interests of the plant and the workers. This effectively overcomes the divide that Drucker found at the base of the plant community.

NOTES

1. Russell L. Ackoff, *The Democratic Corporation*, Oxford University Press, 1994, p. 71.

2. Ibid., p. 72.

3. Ibid., p. 73.

4. E.F. Schumacher, *Small Is Beautiful*, Harper & Row Publishers, Inc., 1973, p. 58. I have had more than one student tell me that they did not have to buy a copy of this book because their father had read it in college.

5. Russell L. Ackoff, *The Democratic Corporation*, Oxford University Press, 1994, p. 78, emphasis in the original.

6. Ibid., p. 78-9.

7. Ibid., p. 79-80.

8. Ibid., p. 89.

9. William Q. Judge, Gerald E. Frexell, and Robert S. Dooley, "The New Task of R and D Management," *California Management Review*, 39, no. 3 (1997); 72-85. Quoted in Leonard Swap, *When Sparks Fly*, p. 202.

10. Tom Peters, forward to *The Art of Innovation:Lessons In Creativity From IDEO, America's Leading Design Firm*, Tom Kelly, Doubleday, 2001.

11. Tom Kelly, *The Art of Innovation:Lessons In Creativity From IDEO, America's Leading Design Firm*, Tom Kelly, Doubleday, 2001, p. 13.

12. Ibid., p. 5.

13. Ikujiro Nonaka, "The Knowledge-Creating Company", *Harvard Business Review on Knowledge Management*, Peter F. Drucker, David Garvin, Leonard Dorothy, Straus Susan, John Seely Brown, Harvard Business School Press, 1998, p. 24.

14. Eileen Appelbaum, Thomas Bailey, Peter Berg, Arne l. Kalleberg, *Manufacturing Advantage*: *Why High-Performance Work Systems Pay Off*, Cornell University Press, 2000, p. 26.

15. Tom Kelly, *The Art of Innovation:Lessons In Creativity From IDEO, America's Leading Design Firm*, Tom Kelly, Doubleday, 2001, pp. 6-7.

16. Ibid., p. 66.

17. Ibid., p. 93.

18. Ibid., p. 75.

19. See the educational film, *The New Face of Work in America*: *Jobs Not What They Used to Be*. Films for the Humanities, 1996.

20. Tom Kelly, *The Art of Innovation*, p. 123.

21. Ibid., p. 140.

22. Eileen Appelbaum and Rosemary Batt, *The New American Workplace*, ILR Press, an imprint of Cornell University Press, 1994, p. 124.

23. Appelbaum et al., *Manufacturing Advantage*, p. 19.

24. Appelbaum and Batt, *The New American Workplace*, p.125.

25. Ibid., p. 126.

26. Ibid., p. 8.

27. Ibid., p. 114.

28. Morton Bahr and William Ketchum, 'Workplace of the Future", *Human Resource Management Journal*, 32, 1993. Cited in Appelbaum and Batt, p. 114.

29. Eileen Appelbaum in personal e-mail.

30. Appelbaum and Batt, *The New American Workplace*, p. 140-1, my emphasis.

31. Ibid., p. 115.

32. Ibid., p. 126-7.

33. *Manufacturing Advantage: Why High-Performance Work Systems Pay Off*, Eileen Appelbaum, Thomas Bailey, Peter Berg, Arne l. Kalleberg, Cornell University Press, 2000, p. 9

34. Ibid., p. 8.

35. Ibid., p. 7.

36. Ibid., p. 8.

37. Jeremy Rifkin, *The European Dream*, Jeremy P. Tarcher/Penguin, 2004, p. 19.

38. *Business Ethics*, Manuel G. Velasquez, 5th, Prentice Hall, 2002, p. 458.

39. *Manufacturing Advantage: Why High-Performance Work Systems Pay Off*, Eileen Appelbaum, Thomas Bailey, Peter Berg, Arne l. Kalleberg, Cornell University Press, 2000, p. 20.

40. Ibid., p. 45.

41. Ibid.

42. Appelbaum and Batt, *The New American Workplace*, p. 118.

43. *Manufacturing Advantage: Why High-Performance Work Systems Pay Off*, Eileen Appelbaum, Thomas Bailey, Peter Berg, Arne l. Kalleberg, Cornell University Press, 2000, p. 53.

44. Ibid.

45. Ibid., p. 54.

46. Ibid., p. 55.

47. Ibid., p. 55-56.

48. Ibid., p. 57.

49. Ibid., p. 58.

50. Ibid.

51. Ibid., p. 59.

52. Ibid., p. 59.

53. Ibid., p. 60.

54. Ibid., p. 69.

55. Ibid., p. 72.

56. Ibid., p. 73.

57. Ibid., p. 74.

58. Ibid., p. 78-9.

59. Ibid., p. 75.

60. Ibid.

61. See "Putting your whole Company's Whole Brain to Work", Dorothy Leonard and Susan Straus, pp. 109-136, Harvard Business Review on Knowl-

edge Management, Peter F. Drucker, David Garvin, Dorothy Leonard, Susan Strauss, John Seely Brown, Harvard Business School Press, 1998.

62. See *Applied Professional Ethics*, Gregory Beabout and Daryl Wennemann, University Press of America, 1994.

63. *Manufacturing Advantage: Why High-Performance Work Systems Pay Off*, Eileen Appelbaum, Thomas Bailey, Peter Berg, Arne l. Kalleberg, Cornell University Press, 2000, p. 76.

64. Ibid., p. 77.

65. Ibid.

66. Ibid., p. 78.

67. Ibid.

68. Ibid., p. 99-100. In this work, the names of the companies that were included in the study were not used. This section refers to "PortableECG1", "PortableECG2", as well as "ECGSystems" as examples.

69. Ibid., p. 115.

70. Ibid., p. 21.

71. Jeremy Rifkin, *The European Dream*, Jeremy P. Tarcher/Penguin, p. 110. The citation from Le Goff is Time, Work, and Culture in the Middle Ages, p. 35.

72. See Jacques Ellul, *The Technological Society*, Vintage, 1967.

73. *Manufacturing Advantage: Why High-Performance Work Systems Pay Off*, Eileen Appelbaum, Thomas Bailey, Peter Berg, Arne l. Kalleberg, Cornell University Press, 2000, pp. 10-11. The reference to Zuboff is *In the Age of the Smart Machine: The Future of Work and Power*, Shoshana Zuboff, New York: Basic Books, 1988. This work applies Howard Gardner's theory of multiple intelligences to an analysis of the workplace changes that occur as information technologies are introduced and the workplace is "informated".

74. Ibid., p. 115.

Chapter VI
Community-Based Economics

Russell Ackoff depicted the social systems view of the organization as being a system that has purposes of its own, it has parts that have purposes of their own, is part of larger systems that also have purposes of their own, and these larger containing systems include other systems that have purposes of their own.[1] So, a business enterprise is really part of a mesh of social relationships that have come to be recognized in contemporary management theory, especially in the stakeholder view of the firm. This recognition of the many interlocking relationships within which businesses operate has made the task of managing a business much more demanding as stakeholders within and without firms are now seen as having a legitimate role in their governance. But, as James E. Post suggests, the recognition of the interlocking of diverse social relationships can introduce needed improvements. "However slightly, capitalism has worked a little better because its practitioners recognized systemic interdependence."[2]

Businesses can make a contribution to a local community by providing jobs, a tax base that may be used to develop the infrastructure of the community, and goods and services that may be consumed locally. But businesses can also have a devastating effect on the larger community if they decide to leave a location for the sake of cheaper labor or more lax environmental standards, for example. This decision leaves people unemployed, causes a deterioration of the tax base, and may thus start a downward spiral in the quality of the infrastructure of a community. That is undoubtedly why Aaron Feuerstein decided not to relocate when his factory burned down in Lawrence, Massachusetts. In response to these challenges, many communities have tried to lure businesses by offering tax breaks and other inducements. They end up bidding against each other, often only to lose a business when the inducements expire. Within the global economy, corporations can easily prey on communities rather than contributing to their stabilization.

Over the last twenty years a new approach to economics has been developing that may be termed community or place-based economics. The goal of this approach is to try to develop strategies that can enable communities to develop their local economies in ways that provide long-term stability. This is not only economically beneficial, but can also contribute to the flourishing of democratic political activity. There is an impressive body of literature that supports the idea that there is an important link between economic and political freedom. As Benjamin R. Barber has observed,

> Democracy clearly depends not only on local social capital but also on local economic capital, not only on the kinds of social trust engendered by civic relations but also on the kinds of economic loyalty spurned by global corporatism, not only on enunciating a market rationale for civics but also on developing a civic rationale for markets. From the perspective of economic efficiency in a global market society, "throwing away" cities whose economies have become "obsolete" may be "rational." But from the perspective of democracy, which depends on the stability, continuity, and economic well-being of the real places where real people live and work, it is insane.[3]

Making a Place for Community analyses the impact of globalization, internal capital mobility, and suburban sprawl on local communities and explores alternative approaches to economic development that have the effect of stabilizing local communities. This approach can be interpreted in light of Heilbroner's view of the last stage in the development of market economies. In the last stage, Heilbroner argued, we have the challenge of selecting among the social opportunities available to us rather than simply responding to economic necessity. Drucker's way of characterizing this task was in terms of the creation of a non-economic society in which economic activity provides a means of achieving some non-economic goal. The approach of community-based economics is to direct economic development toward the creation of democratic communities where persons can flourish as self-governing beings. "Our approach to the question of how to respond to globalization is distinguished from conventional economic discourse in its emphasis on democracy and community as the central frame of reference—not simply economic efficiency."[4]

Job Chasing:

If a social audit were to be carried out on the costs associated with businesses leaving a locality for the sake of inducements offered at another location the result would most often not show a net gain in utility. Applying the public balance sheet approach of David Smith, Thad Williamson et al., indicate that considering the costs associated with the loss of public revenues, increased social spending in the form of unemployment compensation, deterioration of facilities in the vacated location, and increased spending on infrastructure in the new location, etc., leads to the conclusion that policies that contribute to community stabilization would actually be more beneficial overall than competing for jobs by offering inducements that cause businesses to abandon cities, and thus creating throwaway cities. Of course, this approach requires that we consider the effects of a shut down or relocation of a firm from the perspective of the public good and not merely the good of the business alone. From this perspective there are usually "negative externalities related to community economic stability."[5]

Peter S. Fisher and Alan H. Peters point out further that job chasing is not very effective. While it is true that new investments in a community can create jobs,

> To the degree that tax and incentive competition results in a redistribution of jobs, our research lends little or no support to the argument that this redistribution has beneficial effects for the nation as a whole, [by, for example] shifting jobs from places with low unemployment to places with high unemployment...Neither are we persuaded that incentive competition improves locational efficiency.[6]

David Nicklaus finds confirmation of this view in the work of Art Rolnick, the research director at the Minneapolis Reserve Bank. Based on Rolnick's work, Nicklaus observes, "Handing Boeing

$3.2 billion so it will put its new 7E7 assembly plant in Washington State instead of, say, Georgia may look like a good investment from Washington's point of view. But it's a zero-sum game for the nation as a whole."[7] According to Rolnick, "From a national perspective, there are no jobs being gained here...Studies show that most of the companies locate where they were going to go anyway."[8] In addition, an Ohio court found that a $280 million tax break given to DaimlerChrysler in Toledo was unconstitutional since it violated the interstate commerce clause.

Williamson et al., point out that with the development of modern transportation and communication technologies, firm location is not technically determined but socially determined. As Heilbroner suggested, it is now a mater of a social choice, not a mere economic necessity. This opens the possibility of developing economic policies that support the stabilization of communities. It also implies that there need not be an overall loss of efficiency if we were to develop social policies that stabilize communities economically[9]

The problem of developing a comprehensive agenda is not a matter of starting from scratch. Williamson et al., show that there are a number of public policy initiatives in place already that are designed to promote community economic development. Their strategy is merely to extend and coordinate these so that they make up a coherent whole.

In response to the strategy of chasing jobs it would be possible to require that any state receiving federal funds refrain from using those funds to raid jobs from other states. Just such a proposal has been made by Representative Martin Meehan of Massachusetts.[10] This mirrors the "clawback" legislation that some states have adopted to require those who receive inducements or incentives to pay them back if they fail to meet their employment target. In addition, some localities have begun to cooperate to limit the competition to provide inducements for businesses to relocate.[11] But the best approach is to eliminate such inducements altogether in favor of place-based development policies.

> All of the development tools...now used to underwrite conventional corporate-based economic development, often with dubious results, could be used instead to nurture, assist, and expand place-based, com-

munity-stabilizing sectors of the economy....Clearly states have substantial resources available to shape the kinds of economic institutions that flourish within their jurisdiction—money that could instead support community reconstruction.[12]

David Nicklaus notes that Art Rolnick has attempted to eliminate corporate subsidies. In 1999, he persuaded Congressman David Minge to introduce a bill to do so, but it did not go far. As Nicklaus observes,

Perhaps politicians are simply unwilling to act against their own best interests. Every governor, mayor and state senator loves to go on TV and boast about the company that was lured to town with tax dollars. Probably that grateful company will be a source of future campaign donations, too.[13]

Community Stabilization:

There are uses of public money at the federal level that have the effect of anchoring economic development. These include highway spending, the establishment of military bases, state universities, state capitals, and other expenditures like research projects including NASA, for example. Other non-governmental strategies include the development of industrial districts, hub-and-spoke districts, satellite platforms, and state-anchored industrial districts. Williamson et al., point to research that illustrates the effect of business networks and clustering in fixing capital in distinct locations. This is an important consequence of the knowledge economy. Some businesses want to be located in the vicinity of centers of high-technology innovation such as Silicon Valley and the route 128 corridor in Massachusetts.[14] Sites that draw and hold capital because of local beneficial features are said to be "sticky regions"[15]

Of course, where people are able to maintain employment for long periods of time they are also able to develop strong social ties. Membership in clubs and other associations tend to be strong and as a result of the development of this kind of civic culture local democratic participation also tends to flourish.[16]

Williamson et al., provide a review of a range of policies that can support community stabilization beginning with the federal government and moving to local agencies. There are a number of federal programs already in place that are intended to help communities develop economically. These programs seem to run counter to the welter of tax policies and other provisions that foster the destabilization of communities. According to Alice O'Connor, "having encouraged the trends that impoverish communities in the first place, the federal government steps in with modest and inadequate interventions to deal with the consequences…then wonders why community development so often 'fails'".[17]

The first federal policy that Williamson et al., depict is Trade Adjustment Assistance (TAA). This is a policy that provides federal assistance to workers and firms that have been negatively impacted by international trade. Williamson et al., report that in 2002 all forms of trade adjustment assistance totaled $498 million.[18]

For workers, TAA provides benefits in the form of unemployment insurance and training. Indeed, workers are required to enter a training program to receive benefits. Workers also have to show that imports contributed to their being laid off. While there are many flaws in the program, Williamson et al., see it as an important precedent for federal support of the economic development of local communities.

TAA for firms has an even greater focus on communities than the programs available for individual workers. The programs for firms are administered by the Economic Development Administration and are administered by twelve Trade Adjustment Assistance Centers (TAAC).[19] Again, companies have to show that they have suffered a decline in sales, production, or job loss. Firms can receive planning and consulting assistance that can aid them in responding to the decline they have suffered as a result of federal trade policies. The government pays for 75% of the planning and 50% of the consulting service. Firms that have received such assistance tend to survive at a greater rate after five years, they tend to add employees at a higher rate and show stronger sales than companies that have not received such assistance. It is obvious that this kind of governmental policy can have the effect of stabilizing local communities. If we recall the idea of a public balance sheet associated with the costs of moving a company to a new location, it turns out that the costs associated with creating jobs via the trade adjustment assistance programs (keeping firms where they are) are far below the costs associated with relocating. Williamson et al., promote the expansion of such programs in order to stabilize local communities. They also note that this type of trade assistance program is applied after the damage has been done. It would be better to be more proactive in stabilizing the economic development of communities.

Another federal program that is aimed at helping communities adjust to the impacts of trade is the North American Development Bank. Its focus is the impact of NAFTA. Much of the work of the bank is to provide loans that are directed to the development of infrastructure in Mexico and the United States.[20] Williamson et al., note that, as an example, the bank has provided $180,000 in credit to a nonprofit organization in El Paso, La Mujer Obrera through the Community Adjustment and Investment Program to start a restaurant and catering business.[21]

The Workforce Investment Act is a federal program that is not related to trade. It has developed One-Stop centers that provide job training services where workers, trainers, and employers can readily meet. Community Block Grants focus federal dollars on the economic development of communities in a way that decentralizes the decision-making process. Williamson et al., note that informal citizen advisory councils have formed in roughly half of the cities receiving such grants.[22] They are by law to target low-income individuals. It is also fascinating to see that the jobs created by these grants seem to be more stable than those in other typical businesses and tend to employ local residents at a high rate. Closely related to block grants are section 108 loan guarantees and Economic Development Initiative grants. All of these programs indicate the feasibility of developing a unified governmental policy of community based economic development.

Williamson et al., point out that the federal government targets areas in the country that have very high unemployment with federal contracts by designating them "labor surplus areas".[23] Contractors in these areas are given preference in bidding on contracts thus providing economic stimulus to those areas. Similarly, the HUBzone program directs federal dollars to areas of high unemployment, including all Indian reservations.[24]

The Economic Development Administration provides grants to underdeveloped areas. These grants are aimed at infrastructure developments and businesses in areas of persistent high unemployment.[25] The Appalachian Regional Commission is another program that has as its goal the economic development of the Appalachian region. It has been shown that counties within the region covered by the ARC have had greater economic growth than comparable ones outside the region.[26] The Clinton administration modeled its Delta Regional Authority, which aims at the economic development of the Mississippi Delta region, on the ARC.

Another interesting program of note is the Empowerment Zones/Enterprise Communities program. What is of special interest here is the government's requirement that local communities plan their economic development. This strategic planning process is supposed to foster collaboration in the identification of local needs and assets, including the strengthening of communities and retaining certain non-economic values like promoting developments on a human scale.[27] This is precisely the kind of concern Heilbroner identified as being essential to the final stage of economic development. This kind of community oriented economic development represents an attempt to transcend economic necessity in light of the social opportunities that exist within a market economy. For, the local community is able to participate in the decision making process, even as federal dollars are distributed to stimulate local economies. (Could this be seen as being a non faith-based expression of compassion in the market sector?)

Additionally, the government actively targets depressed areas for locating government buildings. This can provide an anchor for employment of local residents with the aim of establishing "healthy vital communities."[28] Williamson et al., are critical of the level of funding for such programs but see them as a model for an expanded use of such strategies to develop communities. The Empowerment Zones/Enterprise Communities program provides a focal point for other federal programs that contribute to community development. They include:

• AmeriCorps USA

• Urban Location Program

• CDBG's

- Substance Abuse Prevention

- John Heinz Neighborhood Development Program

- Planning Program for States and Urban Areas

- Job Opportunities for Low-Income Individuals

- School-To-Work Opportunities

- Youthbuild[29]

What is missing in this plethora of programs is a unified commitment that would provide the coordination as well as the level of funding needed to effectively achieve their goal.

The New Markets Initiative is a new program that was signed into law in December, 2000. It provides tax credits for the creation of "New Market Capital Firms" that will make loans to small businesses. There are forty "Renewal Communities" that are to receive special tax credits for businesses.[30] This may provide a counterweight to the practice of communities to try to outbid each other with tax incentives to attract businesses.

To round out the approaches that can involve the federal government, Williamson et al., depict the reconversion of military bases as a stimulus to community economic development. They report that at some of the military bases that have closed there has been an increase in the number of jobs as a result of targeted economic stimulus.[31] One use for military bases that has beneficial effects for the local community is to convert them into college sites. Colleges are important as anchors for economic development. Military bases are also sometimes transferred to local communities through what is called Economic Development Conveyance.[32] In this case, the land is taken over by a local community which can then convert it into an industrial park, for example.

With all of these programs, and others in addition, aimed at small businesses, transportation and environmental protection, the federal government can play a critical role in developing the economies of local communities, which can in the end contribute to the fostering of democratic activity. For, the civic virtues that are necessary for democratic participation are grounded in a stable local economy.

Public Investment Strategies:

Beyond the federal government, there are a number of policies that state and local governments can pursue to develop their local economies. Some state and local governments have found it useful to run their own businesses as a way of anchoring employment and other spin-off businesses in their locale. This approach can provide some protection to local communities that are vulnerable to disinvestment and may give an incentive for local businesses to remain.[33]

A very traditional area of public ownership in the United States is public utilities. In recent times, many municipalities have become involved in the new telecommunications technologies such as cable television and internet facilities.[34] But Williamson et al., point out that publicly owned enterprises have begun in other non-traditional areas such as banking, real estate, retail merchandising, and energy recovery, such as the methane gas recovery units that attach to some current landfill sites.[35] And Williamson et al., provide evidence of how efficient and profitable these activities are. They certainly come out well according to the public balance sheet approach to assessment discussed earlier. Such publicly owned enterprises not only provide monies in lieu of taxes but can develop new infrastructure and make use of older infrastructure that might otherwise go unused. Of course, publicly owned enterprises can provide support for other private businesses by providing the infrastructure and sometimes training. Williamson et al., note that the development of private telecommunications has been uneven in its geographical distribution since private companies have focused on the urban centers which are most profitable. This is where local governments can step in and fill the void where the market simply considers it unprofitable to provide the infrastructure.[36] A municipally owned telecommunications division of the Tacoma Power Company in Tacoma Washington, Click!'s, was able to attract over 100 high-tech firms to the city within a period of two years.[37] So, these publicly owned enterprises can have significant multiplier effects and provide needed competition.

We have noted that the area of public ownership now includes financial institutions, including banks and insurance companies. This is an important way in which venture capital can be targeted to local economic development. The ownership of real estate allows cities to direct the development of land that is often abandoned by businesses seeking incentives in other localities. Publicly owned land can be leased and thus provide income to the city as well as target the employment of local residents. One example is Alhambra, California, that earns $1 million per year renting a six-acre site to businesses and requires them to reserve a majority of jobs for local residents of low and moderate income.[38] Some cities now own golf courses and retail stores that sell souvenirs. North Carolina purchased a passenger rail line and another freight line which it leased to Norfolk Southern, worth $11 million a year in revenues to the state.[39]

This kind of public ownership is an effective way in which local communities can create jobs and thus stabilize their local economies rather than trying to bribe companies to invest in them. Among the other approaches that cities can use to stabilize their economies are import substitution (finding local substitutes for items imported into the community), buy-local and produce-local strategies, developing local currencies, and economically targeted investments (ETIS) with public pension funds.[40]

Private/Public Investment Strategies:

In addition to public initiatives, Williamson et al., consider private investments that can have a stabilizing effect on local communities. This approach may be contrasted with that of David Schweickart in his study, *After Capitalism*. According to Schweickart's conception, economic democracy implies that there is only public investment (in his pure model). His scheme for economic democracy involves worker control, but not ownership, of enterprises and investment is socially controlled.[41] But Williamson et al., would allow for both private and public investment. It seems clear that private and public investment can complement each other. Indeed, the traditional boundary between private and public sectors seems to break down considerably as municipalities begin to lease public facilities to private companies. For example, the city council of Chicago recently approved the lease of a toll road to a Spanish-Australian consortium for 99 years. It is going to net the city $2 billion.[42]

Another recent development is the movement toward rural sourcing. These are for-profit private companies that sometimes include private-public partnerships. They are aimed at keeping jobs in America and their strategy is to locate in rural areas where costs are lower than in metropolitan areas. Some companies have found that they can employ relatively low-cost IT workers in rural areas of the United States.[43]

Williamson et al., devote a great deal of space to the treatment of employee ownership. This is an approach we have already considered. ESOPs are important for community economic development because such businesses are deeply rooted in place and are unlikely to move solely for economic reasons. In other words, such businesses are liable to take advantage of social possibilities, as Heilbroner suggested, that transcend a bare economic calculus. But Williamson et al., are also interested in the effects ESOPs can have on the democratic participation of its members. Remember that Williamson et al.,'s work is aimed at strengthening the social structures that contribute to democratic participation in the broader society. The rootedness in community that is characteristic of ESOPs is significant in this regard, as well as the civic virtues that can be developed within such an organization as workers take control of their own economic lives. The benefits of ESOPs are both economic and social in character.[44]

The ideal of combining the productivity of capitalist economic methods of production with recognition of the moral standing of the worker is an old one. John Stuart Mill gave expression to this ideal in the nineteenth century. While the moral standard Kant designated a "good will" requires that we ought to treat all persons with respect even if it were not to also make for greater productivity, it is not incompatible with a good will to reap the rewards of the higher productivity that typically follows upon treating persons with respect.

Eventually, and in perhaps a less remote future than may be supposed, we may, through the cooperative principle, see our way to a change in society, which would combine the freedom and independence of the individual with the moral, intellectual and economical advantages of aggregate production; and which...would realize, at least in the industrial department, the best aspirations of the democratic spirit, by putting an end to the division of society into the industrious and the idle, and effacing all social distinctions but those fairly earned by personal services and exertions....[in addition to increasing their productivity Mill thought worker associations would produce a moral revolution]: The healing of the standing feud between capital and labor; the transformation of human life, from a conflict of classes struggling for opposite interests, to a friendly rivalry in the pursuit of a good common to all; the elevation of the dignity of labour; a new sense of security and independence in the labouring class; and the conversion of each human being's daily occupation into a school of the social sympathies and the practical intelligence.[45]

It is in the knowledge economy that has recently emerged that this goal is obtainable because now the knowledge of the worker is the most valuable resource a business has. But the knowledge of the worker is only allowed to be applied effectively within a social structure that also respects them as persons. When we studied Kant's ethical theory in chapter three, we saw that the same demand for freedom in the political sphere applies to the economic sphere. Now we can see that the promotion of economic democracy can support the practice of political democracy. "To the extent that more participatory, job-anchoring institutions continue to expand, place-stabilizing strategies can go hand in hand with the extension of meaningful local-level democracy both at work and in the community."[46]

NOTES

1. Russell L. Ackoff, *The Democratic Corporation*, Oxford University Press, 1994, p. 16.

2. James E. Post, "Perfecting Capitalism: A Systems Perspective on Institutional Responsibility", p. 59 in *Corporations and the Common Good*, ed., Robert B. Dickie and Leroy S. Rouner, University of Notre Dame Press, 1986.

3. *Making a Place for Community*, Thad Williamson, David Imbroscio, and Gar Alperovitz, with a forward by Benjamin R. Barber, Routledge, 2002, Forward, pp. x-xi. Cf., Peter Berger in "The Moral Crisis of Capitalism", "In the same way, just as capitalism clearly cannot be identified with democracy (otherwise one could not explain the cases of capitalist societies with no democracy), there seems to be a propensity of capitalist systems toward democracy." *Corporations and the Common Good*, ed., Robert B. Dickie and Leroy S. Rouner, University of Notre Dame Press, 1986, p. 23. Cf., also Peter Berger's more extended argument along these lines in *The Capitalist Revolution: Fifty Propositions About Prosperity, Equality, and Liberty*, Perseus Books, 1988. Finally cf., *The Democracy Advantage*, by Morton H. Halperin, Joseph T. Siegle, Michael M. Weinstein, Routledge, 2004.

4. Williamson, et al., p. 51.

5. Ibid., p. 13.

6. Fisher and Peters, *Industrial Incentives*, 219. Cited in Williamson, p. 61.

7. David Nicklaus, "Nader lawsuit puts tax incentives on trial in Ohio", *St. Louis Post-Dispatch*, Dec. 12, 2004, G 1.

8. Ibid.

9. *Making a Place for Community*, Thad Williamson, David Imbroscio, and Gar Alperovitz, with a forward by Benjamin R. Barber, Routledge, 2002, p. 16.

10. Ibid., p. 63.

11. Ibid., pp. 63-64.

12. Ibid., p. 64.

13. David Nicklaus, "Nader lawsuit puts tax incentives on trial in Ohio", *St. Louis Post-Dispatch*, Dec. 12, 2004, G 1.

14. *Making a Place for Community*, Thad Williamson, David Imbroscio, and Gar Alperovitz, with a forward by Benjamin R. Barber, Routledge, 2002, p. 66.

15. Ibid., pp. 66-67.

16. We might note that according to Richard Florida, many people in the "creative class" do not work for companies for very long but still identify with places. "Place provides an increasingly important dimension of our identity. Fewer people today find lifelong identity in the company for which they work. We live in a world where many traditional institutions have ceased to provide meaning, stability and support. In the old corporate-driven economy, many people took their cues from the corporation and found their identity there. Others lived in the towns where they grew up and could draw on the strong ties of family and long-term friends." (*The Rise of the Creative Class*, p. 229.) This is

exactly the context in which Peter Drucker introduced his concept of "The Plant Community".

17. Alice O'Connor, "Swimming Against the Tide: A Brief History of Federal Policy in Poor Communities," in Ronald Ferguson and William Dickens, eds. *Urban Problems and Community Development*. Washington: Brookings, 1999, 79-80, cited in Williamson, p. 106.

18. *Making a Place for Community*, Thad Williamson, David Imbroscio, and Gar Alperovitz, with a forward by Benjamin R. Barber, Routledge, 2002, p. 107.

19. Ibid., p. 109.

20. Ibid., p. 110.

21. Ibid., p. 111.

22. Ibid., p. 112-113.

23. Ibid., p. 114.

24. Ibid., p. 115.

25. Ibid., pp. 115-116.

26. Budget of the United States Government, Fiscal Year 1999, 202, quoted in Williamson, p. 116.

27. *Making a Place for Community*, Thad Williamson, David Imbroscio, and Gar Alperovitz, with a forward by Benjamin R. Barber, Routledge, 2002, p. 117.

28. Ibid., p. 118.

29. Ibid., p. 118.

30. Ibid., p. 120.

31. Ibid., pp. 120-121.

32. Ibid., p. 122.

33. Ibid., p. 146.

34. Ibid.

35. Ibid., p. 147.

36. Ibid., p. 151.

37. Ibid., p. 153.

38. Ibid., p. 158.

39. Ibid., p. 163.

40. Ibid., pp. 165-185.

41. David Schweikart, *After Capitalism*, Rowman & Littlefield Publishers, Inc., 2002.

42. "Chicago leases Skyway toll road to foreign consortium", by Michael Dresser, St. Louis Pot-Dispatch, 12/05/2004,
http://www.stltoday.com/stltoday/news/stories.nsf/illinoisstatenews/story/6DEB 19838F52D3CE86256F61004B8572?OpenDocument&Headline=Chicago+leas es+Skyway+toll+road+to+foreign+consortium&highlight=2%2Cconsortium

43. http://www.ccnmag.com/story.php?id=334.

44. *Making a Place for Community*, Thad Williamson, David Imbroscio, and Gar Alperovitz, with a forward by Benjamin R. Barber, Routledge, 2002, p. 192. See Eileen Appelbaum, *Job-Saving Strategies: Worker Buyouts and QWL*, Kalamazoo, MI: W.E. Upjohn Institute for Employment Research, 1989.

45. John Stuart Mill, Principles of Political Economy, (London: Longmans, Green, 1923), Book V, Chapter XI, 791, 189-90. Quoted in Williams, p. 191-192.

46. *Making a Place for Community*, Thad Williamson, David Imbroscio, and Gar Alperovitz, with a forward by Benjamin R. Barber, Routledge, 2002, p. 314.

Chapter VII
The Caring Organization: A New Dream?

We began this study with a consideration of the ideology of compassionate conservatism. We noted that it is difficult to determine exactly what that term is supposed to connote. Is it supposed to differentiate conservatives who are compassionate from those that are not? Does the compassion of conservatives need to be emphasized because they have a reputation for not being compassionate? If conservatives feel the need to express compassion, they ought to be encouraged. In fact, all of us have a moral obligation to be compassionate, not just conservatives. But our compassion need not be restricted to the sphere of private charity. One approach to contemporary management theory attempts to build compassion into the structure of business organizations. It is the so-called Caring Organization. This approach to management is based upon Carol Gilligan's ethic of care. This is an ethical theory that emphasizes human relationships and responsibility. The caring organization is one in which care is:

(a) focused entirely on persons, not "quality," "profits," or any of the other kinds of ideas that much of today's "care-talk" seems to revolve around;

(b) undertaken as an end in and of itself, and not merely a means toward achieving quality, profits, etc.

(c) essentially personal, in that it ultimately involves particular individuals engrossed, at a subjective level, in caring for other particular individuals;

(d) growth-enhancing for the cared-for, in that it moves them towards the use and development of their full capacities, within the context of their self-defined needs and aspirations.[1]

It is obvious that this approach is compatible with the idea of treating persons with respect. If anything, to care may be going above and beyond the call of duty. In this regard, the Care Ethic seems to set too high a standard, much like Kant's ideal of a good will. But, like Kant's ethic, the care ethic can be seen as depicting an ethical ideal toward which we have an obligation to strive. It is certainly a higher ideal than that of the compassionate conservative (or others) who presumably wants to express compassion for the indigent poor but also wants to treat workers as a potential means of cost-cutting. To do so is morally reprehensible because it is not economically necessary. It really represents a social choice, a social possibility. And it is one that does not represent the most intelligent use of technology and social organization in combination.

The caring organization is also an approach that is consistent with the demand for meaningful work and the aesthetic needs of workers in a knowledge economy. The caring organization recognizes that a person's place of work is a primary source of social contact. We make friends with those with whom we work. We may even develop long-term relationships with clients and others outside the workplace who are partners or suppliers, etc. The moving business Two Men and a Truck have as their logo "Movers who Care".[2] The SCOOTER Store, which sells electric scooters and power chairs for the elderly and disabled, advertises that they care about their customers and will spend hours teaching a customer how to operate their scooter. The web site of The Scooter Store advertises itself as having a strong community structure. "Discover how The SCOOTER Store can improve your life when you become a member of The SCOOTER Store family."[3] Of course, the family is the most fundamental model of a community. The SCOOTER Store's core ideology includes many of the elements of a democratized workplace, including worker ownership. It also has the continuous improvement and sense of fun of an innovative organization. It is to be noticed in particular that the improvement of the self as well as the business is emphasized. The two are not mutually exclusive.[4]

Core Ideologies

Always Do The Right Thing
Demonstrate compassion and integrity through words and actions with other employee-owners, customers, families, vendors, neighbors, communities, government agencies, third party payers, competitors and shareholders.

Be Phenomenal
Relentlessly and passionately pursue rapid and continuous improvement for self, other employee-owners and the business.

Grow Aggressively
Build leadership in every market served while expanding rapidly into every viable market.

Focus On The Customer
Focus every person and every department on the relationship to the customer. Strive to exceed the expectations of every customer before, during and after the sale.

Achieve Financial Success
Employee-owners invest intellect, passion and effort to grow ESOP and shareholder value.

Have Fun
Make work fun and celebrate accomplishments large and small.

The idea of the caring organization is one that seems especially suited to the non-profit sector of the economy. But it can provide a model for the for-profit sector as well, especially if we have as our goal to introduce community (and compassion) into the for-profit sector.

There is another similarity between the caring organization and Kant's ethic. We have recalled that Kant's ethic calls on us to act with good will, i.e., we ought to do what is right because it is right. Still, we saw that treating people the way Kant's ethic says they ought to be treated can produce the result of a rise in productivity following on the improved morale of workers who are treated with respect. The same thing is true of the caring organization. While the caring organization is not oriented primarily to profit or other traditional economic goals, it is also true that the environment of a caring organization is usually more conducive to increased productivity. It can also reduce costs by fostering an environment characterized by a high level of trust, reducing absenteeism, the turnover rate of employees, and can also contribute to improved relationships with customers and other external constituents.[5]

There is a fascinating connection between the caring organization and the economic requirements of the knowledge economy.
Eileen Appelbaum and Rosemary Batt have observed that in response to new threats to the competitiveness of traditional high-
volume mass production of standardized goods employing "large
centralized hierarchical organizations, dedicated equipment, and an
unskilled or semi-skilled work force performing repetitive and
fragmented tasks"[6], many firms applied Italian flexible specialization to make production more flexible "through the use of more
flexible technology, combined with the undermining of labor unions, greater use of contingent employment contracts, and the re-
laxation of labor standards governing minimum wages and protec-
tions against arbitrary dismissal."[7] This approach suffered from a
fatal weakness. "Increasing the variety of products increases costs,
and flexible mass production does not improve the ability of firms
to deliver customized products to quality-conscious customers."[8]

In the information economy there is a demand for an economy
of scope as opposed to the traditional economy of scale. An economy of scope is characterized by the production of small batches
of a wide variety of goods in short production runs that can approach individual customization. For example, Dell offers person-
alized computers to order.[9] But this requires that workers be able
and willing to exert discretionary effort for the sake of the firm, to
take the initiative to apply their skills in creative ways to solve
problems as they arise. The caring organization promotes the indi-
vidualization of the work environment implied by this new economic dynamic.[10] The caring organization, in other words, can
increase the worker's commitment to the organization. "Contrac-
tually based relationships do not inspire the extraordinary effort
and sustained commitment required to deliver consistently superior
performance. For that, companies need employees who care, who
have a strong emotional link with the organization."[11]

Velasquez provides an example of a caring organization that
draws interesting parallels to the democratization of the workplace
we have already considered as well as the innovation required in
the knowledge economy. W. L. Gore & Associates, Inc., is famous for its Gore-Tex fabrics. The company's employees practice
self-management which extends to the formation of work teams.
Every employee has a "sponsor" that acts as a sort of coach to help

the employee develop his or her skills and also acts as an advocate in the determination of the employee's compensation by a compensation team. Along the lines of Schumacher's idea that small is beautiful, the company's units are not allowed to grow beyond some two hundred people. This promotes a sense of community within the company since workers are able to develop close personal relationships in such small groups.[12]

The focus on innovation as resulting from the release of the creative freedom of its workers is an explicit theme of GORE-TEX's cultural identity, much like that of IDEO. "Our culture is a model for contemporary organizations seeking growth by unleashing creativity and fostering teamwork."[13] The Gore-TEX internet site that lists employment opportunities reads, "Feeling creative? Enjoy discovery? Like a challenge? Check out our career section."[14] From this perspective, we can see that there is no fundamental conflict between the interests of the firm and those of the workers it employs. This was the divide that Drucker found made the plant community impossible. But in the new knowledge economy such a divide is not economically or socially necessary. "According to Douglas McGregor's Theory Y, 'There is no inherent conflict between self-actualization and more effective organizational performance. If given a chance, employees will voluntarily integrate their own goals with those of the organization'."[15] Here we arrive at the same conclusion as that of Richard Florida in his focus on the development of a creative economy, "Today, for perhaps the first time in human history, we have the opportunity to align economic and human development. Indeed our future economic prosperity turns on making the most of each and every human being's talents and energies."[16]

The new dream of the knowledge economy is to organize the workplace so that the interests of the plant and the workers are aligned. We have seen that this is the promise of high-performance work systems. It is also the promise of the democratization of the workplace. In general, we can say that if capitalism is compatible with community then we can achieve what James E. Post conceived as the perfection of capitalism.[17] But this requires that we see ourselves as a WE rather than an aggregate of I's.[18] According to Appelbaum et al., "Trust in organizations is related to trustworthy behavior by managers...and to the kinds of managerial actions that create an 'ethos of common destiny'."[19] That is a good way to describe a community. It is a social entity in which persons having status share in both the benefits and burdens.

But Appelbaum and Batt have also identified obstacles to the creation of high performance work systems in American firms. Because of the difficulties of making the changes necessary to form a high performance work system, some companies take the easy low-wage route. This is an easy response to the competition from cheap labor abroad. But an important part of Appelbaum and Batt's argument is that U.S. companies cannot compete effectively on this basis. The wages in the developing countries are so low that America simply cannot revert to a wage level that was typical of a century ago. In a race to the bottom America is bound to lose. "The lower limits to which wages can be pushed in advanced industrial economies are well above wages paid in other parts of the world."[20] Pat Buchanan weighs in on this issue in his recent book,

'You can only cut costs so much with new machinery,' says John Monarch, president of GE supplier Smith West. 'Pretty soon you need to lower labor costs, too.' Driessen Aircraft Interior Systems pays Mexican workers $20 a day, which breaks down to $2.50 an hour, less than half the U.S. minimum wage.

If aircraft parts can be made by Mexican workers for $20 a day and computers can be made by Chinese workers for $10 a day, what is there left that cannot manufactured more cheaply abroad? Almost nothing?[21]

The strategy of high performance work systems is for U.S. companies to compete by innovating their work systems to produce high quality products in relatively customized small batches in short production runs. High performance work systems can provide workers with middle-class wages as well as a more enriching work experience and allow them to compete in the world market on the basis of quality and timely production rather than price.

It is also the case that information technology can be used to innovate the workplace or to simply automate it. There is not a technological determinism at work that necessitates the creation of HPWSs along with the adoption of information technology.

As Shoshana Zuboff (1988) has observed, the new technologies can be used either to automate or to informate. That is, they can be used to increase flexibility in some aspects of the production process (scheduling deliveries, controlling inventories) while perpetuating and even intensifying the standardization, specialization, and fragmentation of the work process; or they can be used to transform organizations and to restructure work in fundamental ways....[22]

Managers may have an incentive to avoid innovating the workplace because it would involve a loss of control and perhaps managerial positions. Workplace innovation can result in a flattening of the structure of an organization since workers take on many of the decision making functions of traditional managers. However, in the plants that have adopted a HPWS the managers saw the change as keeping production in the United States. "Many of the managers in the plants that we studied...hoped that HPWSs would allow them to continue to produce goods and employ workers in the United States."[23] On the other hand, the weakness of the union movement in the United States is another obstacle to innovating the workplace. Unions have an interest in forming HPWSs because of the benefits that accrue to their members. Workers are more likely to receive incentive pay in HPWSs. Even if they do not, intrinsic rewards are higher.[24] Unions can also have an influence in saving jobs which might be outsourced or exported overseas.

There is also considerable expense involved in training workers to form a HPWS. Appelbaum and Batt note that executives of firms that are publicly held have been required in recent years to satisfy the demands of stockholders for high dividend payouts which leave little of a company's earnings to apply to the investments needed to innovate the workplace.[25] If stockholders do not receive an adequate return the firm may face a hostile takeover.

Present corporate governance structures in U.S. companies make it difficult for top management to make intra-firm commitments to the development of new production processes or to long-term employment relationships with suppliers. Yet, many researchers have argued that these are the essential characteristics of high-performance production systems.[26]

In order to meet the demands for high payout rates some firms have resorted to downsizing and or outsourcing, as well as vacating job security and gainsharing agreements with their employees.

Finally, Appelbaum and Batt point to the fact that there is no institutional framework for reforming workplaces in the United States. This concern links with the topic of the last chapter. There may be a need for the federal government and local governments to adopt policy changes that will foster innovation in the workplace. The lack of institutional support leads organizations to innovate in a piecemeal fashion. They may try to innovate the workplace at the same time that they try to save costs by downsizing. Without institutional support, companies are tempted to opt for the low-wage response to competition rather than a high-skill one.[27]

The development of an advantageous institutional infrastructure could allow companies to innovate their workplaces proactively, rather than as a response to a crisis situation. Indeed, Appelbaum and Batt point out that a firm may experience a crisis in the process of moving to a HPWS. Low-wage competitors may undercut any advantage they can gain by predatory pricing. A firm that moves to a HPWS is at a disadvantage during a recession if other firms cut costs by laying off workers.

> The lack of legal, bargained, or cultural restrictions on the ability of most U.s. Firms to lay off workers makes it difficult for transformed firms, which rely on mutual trust, to honor their commitments to employment security during periods of recession. Competitors who have not adopted a high-commitment model of work organization will reduce costs during a recession by laying off workers, putting firms that have promised employment security under pressure to renege.[28]

Appelbaum and Batt discuss policy options in several areas that can help firms move to a HPWS. These include improved training institutions, enhanced employee participation, increasing the commitment of firms to their stakeholders, and supporting interfirm collaboration.

In the area of job training, Appelbaum and Batt recommend that job training be directed at both state-of-the-art technology and job reorganization and redefinition. A systemic approach to publicly supported job retraining could focus on firms and workers that are least able to support such training themselves, such as small and medium sized firms.[29] But these are also the firms that create the largest number of jobs. Women and minorities are also constituencies that have a greater need for such support. Large firms could provide matching funds to form a cooperative effort at providing the training necessary for forming HPWSs. States can focus on training in particular areas related to high performance, "training in advanced technologies such as computer-numerically-controlled equipment, in processes such as statistical process control, or in training to enhance total quality and collaborative team work. States such as Illinois and California have already developed some of these alternatives."[30] If training programs are administered by the state, there can develop training networks among community colleges, trade unions, and firms. It would also be possible to develop skill criteria and accreditation requirements for training programs so firms would know what skill sets their employees have in relation to the training they receive.

To facilitate the participation of workers in firms, Appelbaum and Batt recommend the creation of elected employee councils. These are to be modeled on the European works councils and would apply to firms of fifty or more employees. Councils can increase employee participation in both union and non-union settings. ESOPs could be strengthened with appropriate tax subsidies. These policy initiatives together with worker representation on boards provide for a concrete structure that should strengthen worker participation.[31] Additionally, employment security can be reinforced at the state level to enhance worker participation.

The U.S. is the only advanced industrialized country in which employers may hire and fire "at-will". But this employment at-will doctrine has been increasingly challenged in courts over the last decade through tort law, and unjustly-fired employees have won large awards. As a result, one state (Minnesota) has already passed legislation prohibiting unjust dismissal with broad support from the business community; and as of 1991, seventeen other states were also considering such legislation...As in other areas, these state initiatives set an example for the federal government.[32]

Given the examples we saw in the last chapter, it is interesting that Appelbaum and Batt promote regional economic development strategies. They suggest that an officially sanctioned clearing-house be established for the best practices in process technologies and work organizations that employ them. "Such a clearinghouse would help overcome the inherent bias in capital markets against hard-to-monitor investments in human capital. Imperfect information about the impact of such investments in tangibles leads to underinvestment in training and participation."[33]

Because firms in the United States tend to focus on short-term stock price and the short-term return for their shareholders, they often are not able to make the investments needed to create a high performance work system. In order to increase the commitment of firms to all of their stakeholders and promote long-term investments, Appelbaum and Batt recommend a number of policy changes including taxing short-term capital gains at much higher rates than long-term capital gains, introducing a trading tax to dampen speculation, establishing or strengthening laws that regulate hostile takeovers to protect workers, and strengthening stakeholder representation on boards. This last point is compatible with the strategy of the circular organization. They also promote the active participation of workers in directing their pension funds.[34] Overall, the recommendations aim at overcoming external environmental conditions that inhibit the development of HPWSs. Some of these may be seen as market defects within the new knowledge economy. Firms cannot provide all of the conditions for developing HPWSs since the initial costs can be prohibitive. It is necessary for the federal government to establish an environment conducive to it.

HPWSs require greater inter-firm cooperation in training, research and development, and adopting new technologies than traditional mass production systems. Appelbaum and Batt note that some states have already taken steps to facilitate the creation of networks. Jeremy Rifkin's description of the EU's plans for developing new grid technology is rather startling inasmuch as Europe seems to be significantly ahead of the United States in this regard.

Europe's ability to establish unified standards of operation, coordinate activity among competitors, and create public-private partnerships generally gives it a leg up on American companies, where a 'go it alone' strategy often results in competing standards, haphazard development of new technologies, and market redundancies. Certainly this has been the case with the wireless technology revolution and now with the new grid technology.[35]

The state can also establish certification for quality standards. While there already exists an American National Standards Institute and American Society for Quality Control, there is no overarching federal agency to coordinate standards. Here again, Rifkin points out that there are auditing companies that are certified by a number of European governments so as to insure that they meet the quality standards of the Geneva based International Standards Organization.[36]

The last barrier to developing HPWSs is to eliminate predatory pricing by firms that take a low-wage approach to competition. Among the policy proposals in this area are,

> A national health care plan; a national family leave act; the prorating of pension, vacation, and other benefits for part-time workers, the provision of mandated portable benefits for temporary workers; the indexing of the minimum wage; the elimination of tax code provisions and foreign aid program abuses that encourage firms to move production jobs out of the U.S.; and the development [of] international labor standards to accompany trade agreements.[37]

The response of many people in the United States to these proposals will undoubtedly be that you would have us go the way of Europe. "It's socialism!" There is a strong resemblance to the European approach in these proposals. (Although T.R. Reid reports that the Europeans are very rapidly privatizing many areas of their economy that have traditionally been publicly run).[38] By contrast, the low-wage approach of many American firms has resulted in the exportation of many American jobs overseas, stagnation in wages, an increase in poverty in the United States, and a widening gap between the haves and the have-nots. Jeremy Rifkin reports that America ranks 24th among the developed nations in income inequality. He notes that only Russia and Mexico rank lower.[39] At the same time, a comparison of poverty between the United States and the EU is striking. "Seventeen percent of all Americans are in poverty, or one out of every six people. By contrast, 5.1 percent of the people of Finland are in poverty, 6.6 percent in Sweden, 7.5

percent in Germany, 8 percent in France, 8.1 percent in the Nether-
lands, 8.2 percent in Belgium, 10.1 percent in Spain, 11.1 percent
in Ireland, and 14.2 percent in Italy."[40] (A new census report on
poverty was just released as I write this. It shows that poverty
grew by 1.3 million people in the United States in 2003. In addition, the number of people without health insurance rose by 1.4
million).[41]

If we follow the low-wage path in an attempt to maintain the
old mass production model of production it is difficult to see how
wages can rise under the pressure of foreign competition. Corporations will show profits but workers will not make any gains. The
goal of a high performance work system is to reform the workplace
so as to achieve a rise in productivity, a rise in wages, and an improvement in working conditions. The idea is to compete on the
basis of higher quality and on-time production rather than price.
We have seen that some managers see HPWSs as a way of keeping
production in the United States rather than seeking the lowest
wages we can find overseas. The HPWS is not socialism (state
ownership of the means of production), it is a conjunction of capitalism and community. The safety net provisions prescribed by
Appelbaum and Batt represent social conditions that are necessary
for the maintenance of HPWSs. The monies spent on this approach would represent an investment in a coherent economic policy in the context of a knowledge economy.

A New Dream?

In the end, the problem of capitalism and community is the one
that Peter Drucker identified at the time of the Second World War.
An economic system has both economic tasks and social tasks.
According to Drucker, the economic task of capitalistic economies
in the twentieth century was to avoid depressions. We have been
successful in finding ways to do that. But there is, in addition, the
social task of organizing our economic lives in a way that is compatible with our political tradition of free democratic governance.
As Drucker put the issue in 1947,

The chief economic problem of our time—the prevention of depressions—should be solvable by basically mechanical means; by adapting our employment, fiscal, and budgeting practices to the time span of industrial production—that is, to the business cycle. Much more baffling, and more basic, is the political and social problem with which twentieth-century industrialism confronts us: the problem of developing order and citizenship within the plant, of building a free, self-governing industrial society.[42]

While the economic problem of industrial society was resolved by mechanical means, the social problem requires that we make a social choice. One way to avoid making such a choice is to disguise it as an economic necessity that can be resolved mechanically by applying economic laws. But we have seen that there is no economic necessity in using workers as a means of cost-cutting. In fact, there are advantages to not doing so, especially in a knowledge economy. The fact that we no longer live in the age of industrial production is significant for resolving the social problem Drucker found intractable. For, now the idea of the plant community better fits the economic requirements of a knowledge economy.

Jeremy Rifkin's recent book, *The European Dream*, outlines the social choice that the Europeans have made in organizing their new international society, The European Union. Rifkin compares the traditional American Dream with the new European dream that is being encoded in their constitution, which has not yet been ratified. According to Rifkin, the traditional American dream is to win individual freedom by gaining the autonomy that comes with accumulating material wealth. This is why we conceive of progress in terms of an ever expanding standard of living. It may also be why we often end up bowling alone[43] or living in a gaited "community".[44]

The European Dream, on the other hand, involves being embedded in a network of relationships that contribute to a high quality of life. Rifkin summarizes their choice as focusing on "belonging rather than belongings". What is especially interesting about Rifkin's account of the European union is the connection between their new social arrangements and the development of the information society based on new communications technologies. The Europeans have in effect opted for community as a social model reflecting the connectivity of the electronic web, the paradigm of which is the internet. Because economic transactions are so much faster now and global in extent, the old forms of governance are no longer tenable. To maintain the type of corporate governance that was typical of the last century would be comparable to trying to govern the United States using the pony express. According to Rifkin, European businesses see themselves as part of a complex network of relationships that helps to secure their position in the market by spreading risks.[45]

Rifkin marshals a wide range of evidence to argue that the quality of life enjoyed by the Europeans is higher than that enjoyed by Americans. The high quality of life enjoyed by the Europeans is based on a social choice to decrease work and increase leisure time which can be used to build social capital by developing social relationships. The higher productivity of the knowledge economy allows for such a choice. The French now have a 35 hour work week and other countries in the EU are liable to make the same choice. David Schweikart makes an interesting observation in this regard by noting that ecological sustainability requires opting for greater leisure time over consumption.[46] The Europeans have made a social choice to ensure that the basic needs of its citizens are met, including universal health care. These are social goals that reflect the European Union's recognition of the dignity of all persons. According to the constitution of the European Union,

> The Union is founded on the values of respect for human dignity, liberty, democracy, equality, the rule of law and respect for human rights, including the rights of persons belonging to minorities. These values are common to the Member states in a society in which pluralism, nondiscrimination, tolerance, justice, solidarity and equality between women and men prevail.[47]

They are also developing a coherent economic policy based on the connectivity of the electronic network characteristic of the new knowledge economy. It involves considerable cooperation and negotiation between government and business as well as non-profit civil service organizations. Overall, the Europeans see their economic activity as having a non-economic goal. I would say that the goal is the formation of a moral community, a kingdom of ends. The problem they face is demographic. Their population is not growing and so they may not be able to maintain the social supports they have in place, especially with the relatively slow growth rates in their economies.[48] However, there are ways in which the European governments can promote the formation of larger families. For example, in France the government has recently created tax incentives and childcare policies that are beginning to have the effect of increasing the rate of population growth.[49]

The idea of creating a kingdom of ends is the moral foundation of the democratic political tradition. It involves including all of those who are enfranchised or have the status of a citizen. In a way, the development of HPWSs and the democratization of the workplace is an expression of the old American dream, but it simply extends the franchise of ownership to workers, as well as the status of economic citizenship. Remember that many workers today are owners through their pension funds. So, extending participation in the governance of organizations and gain-sharing represents justice. Capitalism and community aims at an effective synthesis of the individualism of the traditional American dream and the enduring human need for community. It is an extension of the American heritage of democratic governance to our economic lives. In the end, the formation of a global knowledge economy has opened the possibility of developing a form of free-market capitalism with a soul, i.e., one that is humane. But it is up to us to see the social possibility before us and choose it.

NOTES

1. Jeanne M. Liedtka, "Feminist Morality and Competitive Reality: a Role for an Ethic of Care?" *Business Ethics Quarterly*, vol. 6, no. 2 (April 1996): 185. Cited in Manuel G. Velasquez, *Business Ethics*, 5th, p. 492. See Richard Florida on the caring organization in *The Rise of the Creative Class*, pp. 130 ff.

2. See http://www.twomen.com/.

3. See http://thescooterstore.com/.

4. See http://www.thescooterstore.com/about_us/MissionandValues.asp?section=about

5. Manuel G. Velasquez, *Business Ethics*, 5th, p. 492. Velasquez cites John Dobson and Judith White, "Toward the Feminine Firm: An Extension to Thomas White", *Business Ethics Quarterly*, vol. 5, no. 3 (July 1995): 466.

6. Eileen Appelbaum and Rosemary Batt, *The New American Workplace*, ILR Press, an imprint of Cornell University Press, 1994, p. 37.

7. Ibid.

8. Ibid.

9. See http://www.dell.com/html/us/products/purely_you/

10. Manuel G. Velasquez, *Business Ethics*, 5th, p. 492-3.

11. C. Bartlett and S. Ghoshal, "Changing the Role of Top Management: Beyond Strategy to Purpose," *Harvard Business Review* (November/December 1994): 81. Cited in Manuel G. Velasquez, *Business Ethics*, 5th, p. 493.

12. Manuel G. Velasquez, *Business Ethics*, 5th, p. 493.

13. http://www.gore-tex.com/webapp/wcs/stores/servlet/ContentFView?storeId=10001&catalogId=10001&langId=-1&productId=10007

14. http://www.gore-tex.com/webapp/wcs/stores/servlet/ContentGView?storeId=10001&catalogId=10001&langId=-1&productId=10005.

15. Eileen Appelbaum, Thomas Bailey, Peter Berg, Arne l. Kalleberg, *Manufacturing Advantage: Why High-Performance Work Systems Pay Off,* Cornell University Press, 2000, p. 30. Quoted in E.H. Schein, *Organizational Psychology*, Engelwood Cliffs, NJ; Prentice-Hall, 1980, p. 68.

16. Richard Florida, *The Flight of the Creative Class*, HarperBusiness, 2005, p. 241.

17. James E. Post, "Perfecting Capitalism: A Systems Perspective on Institutional Responsibility", in *Corporations and the Common Good*, ed., Robert B. Dickie and Leroy S. Rouner, University of Notre Dame Press, 1986.

18. See *The Dynamics of Community*, Sister Marie Beha O.S.F., corpus Books, 1970, "Max Scheler, a German phenomenologist of the early twentieth century, says...man is not only made for communion with other men, he also begins his life experience with the notion of we and only gradually comes to some understanding of the I." Sister Beha cites, Ernst Ranly, *Scheler's Phenomenology of Community* (The Hague: Martinus Nijhoff, 1966), p. 67.

19. Appelbaum et al., *Manufacturing Advantage*, p. 111.

20. Eileen Appelbaum and Rosemary Batt, *The New American Workplace*, ILR Press, an imprint of Cornell University Press, 1994, p. 22. Cf., "How Free Trade Hurts", Byron Dorgan and Sherrod Brown, "But much of the world at the beginning of the 21st century looks a lot like the United States did 100 years ago: Workers are grossly underpaid, exploited and abused, and they have virtually no rights. Many, including children, work 10, 12, 14 hours a day, six or seven days a week, for only a few dollars a day." Washington Post, December 23, 2006, A21.

21. See Pat Buchanan, *Where the Right Went Wrong*, Thomas Dunne Books, St. Martin's Pres, 2004, pp. 165-166.

22. Appelbaum and Batt, *The New American Workplace,* p. 149.

23. Appelbaum et al., *Manufacturing Advantage*, p. 225.

24. Ibid.

25. Appelbaum and Batt, *High Performance Work Systems*: *American Models of Workplace Transformation*, Economic Policy Institute, 1993, p. 48.

26. Ibid., p. 49.

27. Ibid., p. 57.

28. Ibid., p. 59-60.

29. Ibid., p. 62.

30. Ibid., p. 63.

31. Ibid., pp. 64-5.

32. Ibid., p. 66.

33. Ibid.

34. Ibid., pp. 68-9

35. Jeremy Rifkin, *The European Dream*, Jeremy P. Tarcher/Penguin, 2004, p. 48. See *The United States of Europe*, T. R. Reid, Penguin Press, 2004. Thomas Friedman has reported that the United States has fallen to 16th in the world in wireless connectivity. See "Calling All Luddites", http://www.nytimes.com/2005/08/03/opinion/03friedman.html?

36. Jeremy Rifkin, *The European Dream*, pp. 69-70.

37. Appelbaum and Batt, *High Performance Work Systems*: *American Models of Workplace Transformation*, Economic policy Institute, 1993, p. 70.

38. T. R. Reid, The United States of Europe: The New Superpower and the End of American Supremacy, p. 124, "For all its devotion to governmental programs and the welfare state, Europe stands ahead of the United States in the drive to privatize traditionally governmental operations. Passenger rail service, still the province of taxpayer-funded Amtrak in the United States, has been turned over to private companies in most of Europe. Some countries are handing over air traffic control and tax collection to the private sector."

39. Jeremy Rifkin, *The European Dream*, p. 38.

40. Ibid., p. 40.

41. http://www.chicagotribune.com/business/chi-0408270108aug27,1,4982726.story?coll=chi-news-hed

42. Peter Drucker, "Henry Ford: The Last Populist", first published in *Harper's Magazine*, 1947, reprinted in *The Ecological Vision*, Transaction Publishers, 1993, p. 45.

43. See Robert Putnam, *Bowling Alone: The Collapse and Revival of American Community*, Simon & Schuster, 2000.

44. Jeremy Rifkin, *The European Dream*, p. 155.

45. Ibid., p. 190.

46. David Schweikart, *After Capitalism*, Rowman & Littlefield, 2002, p. 15.

47. http://gandalf.aksis.uib.no/%7Ebrit/EXPORT-EU-Constitution/Draft-EU-Constitution-June-2004/Article I-02.html.

48. And yet, Robert J. Samuelson reports that some European economies have recently been increasing their rates of productivity, "A brighter spot is Europe, where domestic growth is accelerating. From 2001 to 2005, annual growth in the euro zone (the 12 countries using the euro) averaged only 1.4 percent. Now the OECD forecasts 2.2 percent in 2007 after 2.6 percent in 2006—and that might go higher.", in *Newsweek*, "Rebalancing the Economy", December 25, 2006, p. 52.

49. See "As Europe Grows Grayer, France Devises a Baby Boom", by Molly Moore, Washington Post Foreign Service, October 18, 2006; Page A01.

Select Bibliography

Ackoff, Russell L., *The Democratic Corporation*, Oxford University Press, 1994.

Appelbaum, Eileen, *Job-Saving Strategies: Worker Buyouts and QWL*, Kalamazoo, MI: W.E. Upjohn Institute for Employment Research, 1989.

Appelbaum, Eileen, with Thomas Bailey, Peter Berg, Arne l. Kalleberg, *Manufacturing Advantage: Why High-Performance Work Systems Pay Off*, Cornell University Press, 2000.

_____. *High-Performance Work Systems: American Models of Workplace Transformation*, Economic Policy Institute, 1993.

_____ *The New American Workplace*, ILR Press, an imprint of Cornell University Press, 1994.

Bauman, Z., *Community: Seeking Safety in an Insecure World*, Cambridge: Polity, 2001.

Bender, Thomas, *Community and Social Change in America*, The Johns Hopkins University Press 2000.

Berle, Adolf A., *The 20th Century Capitalist Revolution*, Harcourt, Brace; [1st ed.] edition, 1954.

Berle, Adolf A., Means, Gardiner C., *The Modern Corporation and Private Property* Transaction Publishers; Reprint edition 1991.

Bowie, Norman, *Business Ethics: A Kantian Perspective*, Blackwell Publishers, 1999.

Daly, Herman E., and John B. Cobb, Jr.; with contributions by Clifford W. Cobb, *For the Common Good : Redirecting the Economy Toward Community, the Environment, and a Sustainable Future*, Beacon Press, 1994, 2nd ed.

Davis, Stephen, Jon Lukomnik, David Pitt-Watson, *The New Capitalists: How Citizen Investors Are Reshaping the Corporate Agenda*, Harvard Business School Press, 2006.

Dickie, Robert B., Rouner, Leroy S., ed., *Corporations and the Common Good*, University of Notre Dame Press, 1986.

Dowd, Douglas, F., "Amartya Sen: The Late Twentieth Century's Greatest Political Economist?", in *Understanding Capitalism: Critical Analysis from Karl Marx to Amartya Sen*, London, Sterling VA., Pluto Press, 2002.

Drucker, Peter F., *The Ecological Vision*, Transaction Publishers, 1993

_____. *The End of Economic Man*, The John Day Company, 1939.

_____. *A Functioning Society: Selections from Sixty-Five Years of Writing on Community, Society, and Polity*, Transaction Publishers, 2003.

_____. *The Future of Industrial Man*, The John Day Company, 1942.

_____. *Concept of the Corporation*, New York, Mentor Book, 1972.

_____. *The New Society*, New York, Harper & Row, 1962.

_____. *Post-Capitalist Society*, New York, HarperBusiness, 1993.

_____. *Technology, Management, and Society*, Harper & Row, 1977.

Dudley, Kathryn Marie, *The End of the Line: Lost Jobs, New Lives in Postindustrial America*, Chicago: University of Chicago Press, 1994.

Ehrenreich, Barbara, *Nickel and Dimed: On Not Getting By in America*, Owl Books, 2002.

Etzioni, Amitai, *The Moral Dimension: Toward a New Economics*, Free Press, 1990.

Ewing, David W., *Freedom Inside the Organization*, E. P. Dutton, New York, 1977.

Florida, Richard, *The Flight of the Creative Class*, HarperBusiness, 2005.

_____. *The Rise of the Creative Class*, Basic Books, 2004.

Fukuyama, Francis, *Trust: The Social Virtues and The Creation of Prosperity*, Diane Pub Co, 2000.

Greider, William, *The Soul of Capitalism: Opening Paths to a Moral Economy*, Simon & Schuster, 2003.

Guillet de Monthoux, Pierre, *The Moral Philosophy of Management : From Quesnay to Keynes*, M.E. Sharpe, c1993.

Halperin, Morton H., Joseph T. Siegle, Michael M. Weinstein, *The Democracy Advantage*, Routledge, 2004.

Hargadon, Andrew, *How Breakthroughs Happen: The Surprising Truth About How Companies Innovate*, Harvard Business School Press, c2003.

Harrison Thad, et al., in *Making a Place for Community*, Routledge, 2002.

Heilbroner, Robert A., *The Future as History*, Grove Press, Inc., 1961.

_____. *The Making of Economic Society*, Prentice Hall; 11 edition, 2001.

_____. *The Worldly Philosophers: The Lives, Times And Ideas Of The Great Economic Thinkers*, Touchstone; 7th Rev edition, 1999.

Herbrechter, Stephan, and Michael Higgins, eds., *Returning (to) Communities: Theory, Culture, and Political Practice of the Communal*, Rodopi, 2006.

Kelly, Tom, with Jonathan Littman, *The Art of Innovation*, New York : Doubleday, 2001.

Mayo, E., *Social Problems of an Industrial Society*, Andover, MA: Andover Press, 1945.

Nisbet, Robert, *The Quest for Community*, New York, Oxford University Press, 1977.

Olasky, Marvin, *Compassionate Conservatism*, The Free Press, 2000.

Reid, T.R., *The United States of Europe: The New Superpower and the End of American Supremacy*, Penguin Press, 2004.

Rifkin, Jeremy, *The European Dream*, Jeremy P. Tarcher/Penguin, 2004.

Samuels, Warren J., Edward, ed., *New Horizons in Economic Thought: Appraisals of Leading Economists*, Elgar Publishing Company, 1992.

Schor, Juliet B., *The Overspent American*, Perennial, 1999.

Schumacher, E.F., *Small Is Beautiful*, Harper & Row Publishers, Inc., 1973.

Sen, Amartya, *On Ethics and Economics*, Blackwell Publishing, 1988.

Stewart, Thomas A., *The Wealth of Knowledge: Intellectual Capital and the Twenty-First Century Organization*, New York : Currency, 2001.

Swap, Leonard, *When Sparks Fly*, Harvard Business School Press, 1999.

Turkle, Sherry, *Life on the Screen*, Simon & Schuster, 1997.

Uchitelle, Louis, *The Disposable American: Layoffs and Their Consequences*, Knopf, 2006.